C O N T E N T S

Foreword

By Jay Thadeshwar

I am delighted to write this foreword, not only because Karthik Krishna has been a friend and colleague for so many years, but also because I believe deeply in the educative value of the concepts in this book for all the readers, especially in today's times of uncertainty.

I run a digital advertising agency established in 2015 with the purpose of empowering MSMEs by introducing the perks of digital world to them. We have served over 250 brands in the last 5 years which belong to various types, sizes and industries. From bootstrapped startups to some of the leading international brands, we have worked with them all. We have managed marketing efforts for some of Karthik's ventures. He has a very unique ability to quickly identify widely faced but rarely addressed problems and analyze their scale. He would keep the agenda of our meetings aside and discuss random problems and probable solutions. This has led him to create many successful ventures at a very young age. I wasn't surprised when he called me about this book. Like any other industry professional I had admired the problem too but he acted upon it and wrote this book. That's Karthik for you.

I also believe that even Entrepreneurs at every level and stage of their career can enrich and strengthen their foundations by learning the patterns and practices presented in this book.

In my journey of professional life, I have observed many small businesses wanting to go online and run at least a part of their operations online but due to limited tech knowledge and budget, they can't. Most of the time they don't know how to start, where to look and who to ask. This book addresses all those 3 issues.

You're now holding or viewing Karthik's next big project, and I couldn't be prouder of it. Building on the practices and observations from his remarkable journey, The $100 Heist will inspire you and spark your journey.

Most books in this space are written by someone who had a winning-lotto-ticket idea, but how many of us can really hope to realize the same success? Karthik doesn't teach you how to get rich quickly—he teaches you how to get rich correctly. His book provides sustainable and accessible methods for the rest of us. Indeed, success is a foundation with many pillars, and each pillar, from mindset to networking to health, must be solid. Karthik helps you build solid pillars through actionable success principles.

In this book, Karthik explains how to build your plan around a core strategic combination of market, identity, and focus. I like the idea that the real plan is not the output format, but what's supposed to happen, and why, and when, and how much money. It's ideas like this that make me say that everybody has an entrepreneur hidden inside them, but only in the simple, pragmatic context that this book evangelizes. And that's why you should buy this book.

It is my hope and expectation that this book will provide an effective learning experience and referenced resource to all the hustlers, dreamers, Wantrepreneurs and Entrepreneurs out there.

Introduction
The Golden Age of Entrepreneurship

IF YOU HAVE PICKED UP this book, it's more than likely that you identify — or would like to identify — as an entrepreneur. You didn't grab this book by accident; you're destined for this journey.

With this book in hand, nothing can hold you back. You are going to learn how to master the three concepts that will catapult you to the success you deserve:

1. Opportunity
2. Knowledge
3. Execution

Once you master these three concepts, you can almost effortlessly become the highly successful, financially independent entrepreneur you are meant to be.

> **"A pessimist sees the difficulty in every opportunity;**
> **an optimist sees the opportunity in every difficulty."**
> - Winston S. Churchill

Opportunity

The first piece of the puzzle is Opportunity. No matter where you live or what you do, remember that you are surrounded by opportunities on a daily basis. According to a recent article in Forbes, there are almost 28 million small businesses in the United States alone. Over 22 million of these businesses are made up of self-employed individuals with no payroll or employees.

When most people think about launching a small business, their minds naturally gravitate toward the idea of "traditional" small businesses. The truth is that 52% of small businesses are home-based - and a whopping 15 million people have a business.

What's even more intriguing is that approximately 543,000 new businesses are started every single month! The technological advances we have experienced in the 21st century provide us, as entrepreneurs, with far more opportunities than ever before. Why? Because the world as a whole is now a single market.

This means that entrepreneurs can now think about opportunity on a global scale from Day One, yet they can start locally. This approach, known as globalization, means that you can design and deliver global solutions that have relevance to every local market you plan to target.

Look at a social media platform like Instagram, for example. Many people around the world are making a fortune simply by posting pictures online. That's it. All they are doing is posting pictures online, and big brands are fighting to find them and pay them to endorse their products.

Why? Because these Instagram (or YouTube) superstars are a "face" that their buyers will recognize... and as you know, recognition means money and sales. Lots of it.

The concept is simple: Take pictures, get thousands of followers, and make money. That's why it's called an opportunity.

Take Pictures   Get Thousands   Make Money
                     of Followers

With today's key social media platforms, an entrepreneur can create a product, build a reputable brand, and grow a new business. You can now do all this with very low upfront costs and a high level of interactivity with potential clients and customers. This was never before possible. These social media platforms provide communication, mobilization, and location-based services.

Another opportunity that can be just as profitable is to create your own website. You may be thinking, "Sure, a website would be awesome, but it's too hard to get started and to convert it into something financially viable."

While it might seem overwhelming, in this book I am going to prove to you how you can become a very profitable businessperson simply by creating a website.

Regardless of your niche, the cost of entry for a startup is at an all-time low. Ten years ago, creating a website for e-commerce would easily require a million dollar investment. Today, however, you can create a website for next to nothing and be on your way. And if you want to expand a little further, smartphone applications can be built for less than a couple thousand dollars. That means you can invest in your own business with no need for an outside investor!

What does all of this mean?

Well, if you are ready to get out of the 9 to 5 grind, become a highly successful entrepreneur, and embrace financial freedom, then this book is for you.

This book will provide you with the insider information that you can utilize to make that goal a reality. But please, please read this book to the very end and take each and every action I ask of you. This is imperative to your success because this book gives you the proven blueprints and strategies that you can copy and use to create your own profitable business right out of the gate!

Now, I'm not guaranteeing that you are going to start making six figures, seven figures, or even eight figures a year. What I can guarantee is that if you take action and execute every single step within this book, you will become a very successful entrepreneur.

It all goes back to the global market I mentioned earlier. With the world now a single market, all you need to start your journey to success is access to a laptop and the internet. That's it.

With a laptop and the internet, your area of opportunity includes more than just your local market; your opportunity is truly global. That's right. You can reach a global market working from anywhere: your home office, your living room, or even your neighborhood coffee shop!

It's all about opportunity, and in today's world, opportunities continue to grow.

Think about it. Ten years ago, if you were going to quit your 9 to 5 job to become an entrepreneur, you would have had a very difficult time. For many individuals it was nearly impossible. Jobs weren't the same even ten years ago.

As I write this in 2020, I am confident that things will change even more in the coming decade. It's very likely that 30% of the jobs that exist in today's economy will slowly disappear, and the new generation will be offered an entirely new world of opportunity. And our grandchildren? They will have jobs that we never imagined would exist because opportunity will continue to increase.

Because opportunity continually increases, you can invest a small amount right now to start building a profitable business. In this book, I am going to share with you a specific strategy that will show you how to turn a one-hundreddollar bill into a profitable business.

You might be thinking, "Well, this is basically geared toward millennials and Generation Y; young kids who can embrace technology and really understand the new languages being used on the internet." This is entirely incorrect - a false mentality that many people have. It's also the same mentality that quite often deters success!

The truth is that Baby Boomers are joining the fun in record numbers. The percentage of Baby Boomer entrepreneurs starting a business grew from 14.3% in 1996 to 23.4% last year. In fact, in every one of the past 15 years, Boomers between the ages of 55 and 64 have had a higher rate of entrepreneurial activity than Generation Y - and every year their numbers grow more. I have had many successful Baby Boomers read this book and apply it, going on to generate millions online.

Regardless of your age or technical background, following the system and blueprint you are about to learn in this book can help you become a successful entrepreneur. You simply need to believe in yourself and trust the process that's laid out in this book.

My strategy and blueprint work whatever your knowledge or experience. What I'm sharing with you is easy and the opportunity is massive. In fact, the opportunity I'm about to show you in this book will be worth half a trillion dollars by 2021. Even a tiny 0.000001% of that is still a six-figure business — the same as what a doctor earns every year.

Knowledge

You now understand that opportunity is all around you, and that this book is also an opportunity. However, in order for you to embrace this or any opportunity in the future, you need to have the second concept in line: Knowledge.

> **"The greatest enemy of knowledge is not ignorance.**
> **It is the illusion of knowledge."**
> - Stephen Hawking

The 21st century has surrounded us with knowledge. It is no longer necessary to grab the trusty Encyclopedia Britannica to become knowledgeable about a particular topic. Instead, all we need to do is a quick online search. The wealth of information on the internet is enormous. You can use it to apply new knowledge, learn a new skill set, and take one step closer to becoming a successful entrepreneur.

Without the internet, you would either

a) Have to go to school, or

b) Pay a fortune for a mentor who would show you exactly what you need to do to become a success.

Because of today's easy access to information, you have many opportunities to obtain knowledge: from a Google search, watching Youtube videos, or attending an online webinar. Webinars are great tools which provide you with targeted knowledge in one convenient place.

When I first got started, I was just as lost as you must be right now. To gain my knowledge, I had to travel around the country, spending a lot of money per trip to attend seminars. Now, thanks to webinar technologies, all you have to do is grab a laptop, click a webinar button, listen to the training, and bam! You are all the wiser.

At the next level, consider all the colleges and universities that now offer web-based learning. There is often no need to travel or even leave your house to learn. Instead, you can simply log in to a virtual classroom from the comfort of your own home.

No matter what niche or industry interests you, it is important to start gaining as much knowledge as you can. In your case, this means learning how to efficiently build an online business. The knowledge that you are going to gain in this book will provide you with every tool you will need to make that happen.

The more knowledge you acquire, the more successful you will be in the long run. Alternately, if you don't embrace this knowledge you will never be successful

Execution

Great entrpreneurs didn't just acquire knowledge. They executed it! Execution is one of the most important pieces of the puzzle leading to your success.

Why? Consider this: Even if you are surrounded by a wealth of knowledge and multiple opportunities, they are worthless if you don't execute them. You need to focus and execute. While you're reading this book, for example, I want you to execute everything I ask you to execute. Don't just read the words on the page. Apply what you learn.

This is how you will get from zero to success on the internet. Follow my book step-by-step and you will have the ability to create a six- to seven-figure business and to live the life of your dreams.

All I ask is that you give up your TV time and spend at least one hour per day applying what I show you in this book. If you do that and follow my lead, you will gradually succeed. Without opportunity, knowledge, and execution, you cannot have a successful business.

As you move on to Chapter 1 of this book, I want you to promise me that you are going to execute every single step I show you. That way I can help you launch and build a profitable business that puts you on the path to becoming the successful entrepreneur you were meant to be.

Chapter 1

The 1000 Feet Overview

Turn A Hundred Dollar bill Into
A Profitable E-Commerce Business

SAY WHAT? Yes, you read that correctly. By the end of this book, I am going to show you just how you can successfully turn a $100 bill into an e-commerce business of which you can be proud.

Not only that, but the business you create will flourish once you have learned how to embrace the opportunity, implement the knowledge you have learned, and execute it accordingly.

It's all part of the money-making puzzle I mentioned in Chapter 1. Throughout the rest of this book, you will have the opportunity to make micro-investments, each of which will help bring you one step closer to your end-game of becoming a financially free, successful entrepreneur.

Now, when I say "micro-investments," I mean you can invest $10 at a time. Everything combined will total less than $100. By the time you finish investing that $100, I can virtually guarantee that you will have your e-commerce business up and running.

Still don't believe me? Take out a piece of paper and write down the amount of money I ask you to invest. By the end of the book, you will see that you have invested less than $100. Think about that for a second. For less than the cost of your monthly cable bill, you can launch your new business. Madness, right? Well, it's the kind of madness that you're going to be able to monetize and take to the bank.

Not much more than a decade ago, it was impossible to turn $100 into a viable business. Back then you'd have to spend thousands before even seeing your first customer. And forget about an online business. It used to cost a fortune to have a simple website, let alone an e-commerce business. A basic website could easily cost $100,000. And an e-commerce site? Upwards of one million dollars!

This is **not an exaggeration!**

To save money, many people decided to learn how to create websites themselves. This required a lot of confusing coding and complicated programming. It took years to learn how to implement a solid design, code the site, and program it to be functional. You had to add the code to NotePad and then utilize something called Netscape Communicator to view the success of the code, which almost never worked (for newbies, anyway).

Thankfully, today you can have that e-commerce business for less than $100 without having to stress about code or any other technicalities. And that $100 is loose change in comparison to the millions people used to pay.

When I reflect back on how I started on the internet, I clearly remember it taking me more than two years to learn everything I needed to know to create a website. By the time I was creating websites, I was charging clients loads of money because that was the only way I could create a lucrative business. Back in those days, designers and programmers could make a fortune by creating simple websites. That is not the case today.

Thanks to rapidly-evolving technology, today anyone can create a sleek, functional website for free. You can use platforms like WIX or WordPress to create a website in just a few hours for nothing or next to nothing! You don't need to invest a fortune.

You can launch an e-commerce business for under $100 and I am going to show you how.

Now, in order for you to turn that website into serious profit, there is a five-step system that you will need to follow, one that can help you go from zero to profit in no time and within $100. This concept is essentially why I decided to call this book **The $100 Heist**.

What's great about my **Five-Step Framework to Success** is that you don't need any prior knowledge or experience. I am going to hold your hand and guide you all the way through each step. All you need is a desire to succeed and you will be on your way to generating the profitable business you have been dreaming about for years.

In this chapter, I am going to briefly discuss these five steps and how they work. Later in the book, I will go into depth on each step so that you can become a master of executing this blueprint and launching your profitable e-commerce business.

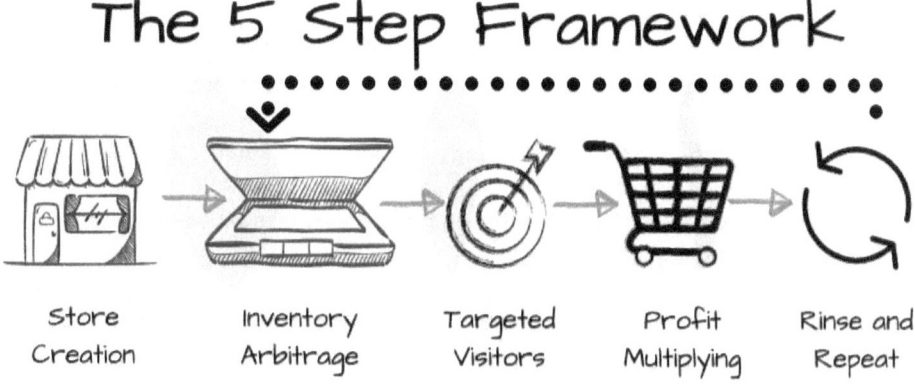

The 5 Step Framework

| Store Creation | Inventory Arbitrage | Targeted Visitors | Profit Multiplying | Rinse and Repeat |

Step 1: A Website Store Is a Must

Some people find this step intimidating because they believe that they don't have enough knowledge or experience to create a website. If this doubt has popped into your mind, remember that we are in a technologically driven era which offers you a million and one ways to make this happen. As I mentioned earlier in this book, I am going to show you specific technology that you can use to create your own e-commerce website in no time at all and with little investment.

In fact, you don't need to have any knowledge about programming or design. All you need is a computer, access to the internet, and the ability to type in some words or copy and paste. If you can manage that, you will have your website up and running by the end of this book. Better yet, you will become a master at building these websites. The sky is the limit.

Step 2: Inventory

Once you have traffic and your website, you will need inventory. After all, an e-commerce website without inventory is like a bird without feathers: You'll get nowhere, really fast.

To be more specific, you need what I call Inventory Arbitrage. I am going to show you how to gain access to millions of products without spending tons of money. In fact, I will show you how to gain access to these products with zero capital. Yes, for free.

I'm going to share the secret that has made it possible for me to build online marketplaces with hundreds and thousands of products - products that I have never actually seen in person. In Chapter 5 of this book, I am going to guide you through the process of this very unique strategy. I will also give you complete access to millions of products, including top brands like NFL and NBA products and more. This winning blueprint will be yours later on in this book.

Step 3: Traffic Makes Perfect

No matter what your background is, you probably understand the importance of website visitors. Without visitor traffic, you have nothing, so the first thing you need to know is how to attract visitors to your website. And not just any website visitors; what you want and need is targeted website traffic made up of people who are actively interested in and looking for what you are offering.

If you have high-quality (targeted) visitors, you will make more money. It is as simple as that. Later in this book, I will share a strategy of mine that you can utilize to access billions of visitors and direct them to your website. Obviously, without visitors your website won't generate a profit. That's why Step 1 - setting up a website store - plays a critical role in my 5-Step System to Success.

Step 4: The Profit Multiplier

Leveraging your traffic and inventory is key when it comes to your website making more money and growing exponentially. In this step, I will share with you the specific strategies that have elevated my brands and multiplied my profits time and time again.

Step 5: Scale Up, Then Rinse and Repeat

Once you have mastered Step 4, it will be time to scale up and repeat the process. Scaling up, then rinsing and repeating, is an important key to success. Why? Because creating multiple streams of income means serious moneymaking potential. There is no limit to the number of stores you can create. After you do this, you can generate more targeted traffic.

Imagine you have five different e-commerce businesses which each generate ten thousand dollars in profit per month. That equals $50,000 a month in profits — entirely reachable if you follow my framework.

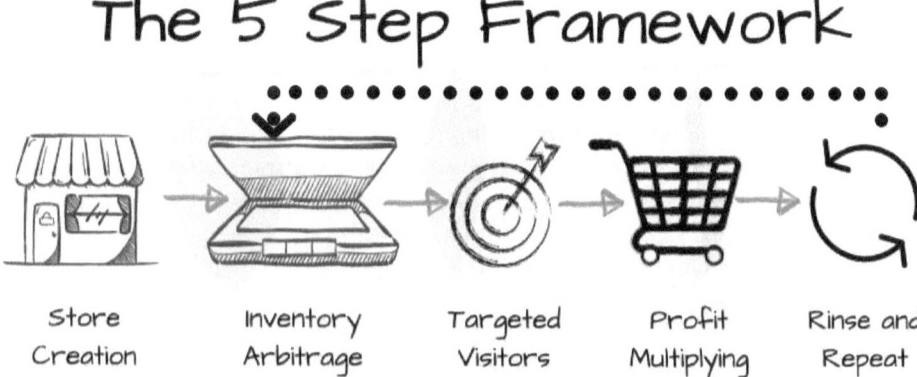

The 5 Step Framework

| Store Creation | Inventory Arbitrage | Targeted Visitors | Profit Multiplying | Rinse and Repeat |

In this book, I share several vital points with specifics on what to watch when you are scaling up your business, and then rinsing and repeating the process. These strategies show exactly how to avoid nasty pitfalls that can cost more than your profits can cover.

Just think. In only a few months' time, you could be the owner of a half-million dollar business.

Throughout the rest of this book, I lay out the entire blueprint on how I use this 5-Step System to Success to create a profitable e-commerce store starting with less than $100. In the pages that follow, I will prove to you that you can do this, and that everything I talk about in this book will soon be your reality - if you execute everything I share.

Chapter 2

Your Opportunity Within Falling Empires

Retail is going Downhill

IN 1995, AMAZON SOLD ITS VERY FIRST BOOK ONLINE. It wasn't long before WaldenBooks, B. Dalton, and Media Play went out of business. Borders Bookstores closed in 2011. Barnes and Noble's sales have declined for years, and its prospects for survival past 2019 are shaky at best. [1]

Since the inception of consumer sales on the internet, brick-and-mortar retail giants have closed stores at an increasing rate every year. The list of casualties grows every time you watch the news. Walmart. Target. J.C. Penney. It's like witnessing the fall of the Roman Empire.

This retail apocalypse is now in its full throes. Fox Business reports that Macy's, Abercrombie & Fitch, Gymboree, HHGregg, Michael Kors, The Gap — even CVS and Victoria's Secret — continue to shutter hundreds of stores in the U.S. and around the world. The Limited and Payless Shoes have now closed all of their physical stores. And Sears/KMart, Toys R Us, American Apparel, BCBG, and Bon-Ton have all filed bankruptcy. [2]

What's the deal?

What is going on to make these retail giants - stores we have relied upon for decades - close more and more stores every year?

For one, the cost of employees, real estate, and inventory are increasing year after year. These increasing overhead costs are sabotaging brick-and-mortar retailers. The more their costs rise, the more vulnerable they are.

But the destruction of traditional retail brands goes deeper than just expenses. Rising overhead cost is only one of the problems for these companies.

The real issue for them is the global trend of consumers purchasing from online retailers. This is what we call e-commerce.

While major retailers watch their sales plummet and are forced to shutter stores, online retail sales continue to sky rocket. It truly is unfortunate that many of these brick-and-mortar retailers are laying off employees. (If you work for a retail chain, I would suggest that you either find a new job or start wearing a new hat: the hat of entrepreneurship.)

Even so, not all major retailers are giving up!

Many are catching on and shifting their focus to e-commerce. Every single major retailer is now investing money and infrastructure into e-commerce because it is the reality of retail in the 21st century.

In fact, e-commerce continues to grow exponentially. According to Business Insider, retail giant Target is now focusing heavily on online sales. Originally, Target had planned to expand their presence in Canada. They mistakenly thought they could gain market share and increase sales by expanding into another country. In less than one year after opening, every single Canadian Target store was forced to close, leaving empty stores all over Canada and causing the layoff of thousands of employees.

Why? Consumers are now geared toward purchasing online.

Let's face reality. People are becoming more comfortable with shopping online. Why leave home when you can do so much on your smartphone or laptop? You can compare prices online. You can find product reviews online. You can find similar products online. There are just so many reasons a consumer would rather shop online. In fact, many stores, such as Best Buy, have a lot of deals that are exclusive to online sales only.

This is where the trend is going. It is the reality of retail right now. And this is where opportunity comes into play - for the big guys, yes, but there is also a huge opportunity for you.

Consumers are now confident enough to take out their credit card, enter that magical 16-digit number on their computer, tablet, or phone, and make a purchase.

Best of all, this online shopping trend gives you an enormous advantage!

Unlike large retailers, you have few, if any, overhead costs when operating an online retail store, also known as an e-commerce website. If you apply the 5-Step System laid out in this book, it will allow you to start raking in your piece of the pie from the half-a-trillion dollar retail industry.

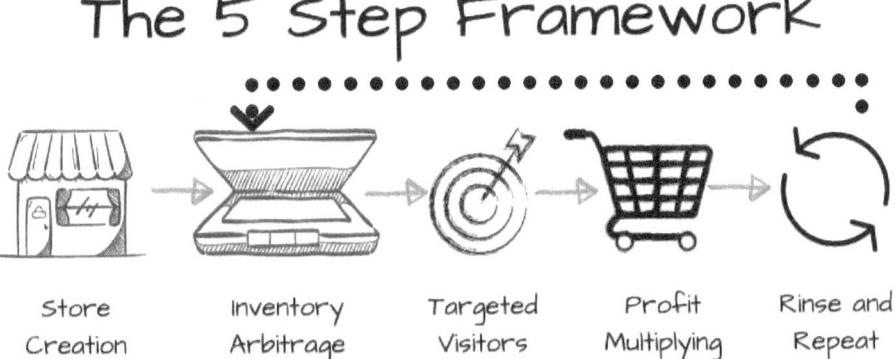

| Store Creation | Inventory Arbitrage | Targeted Visitors | Profit Multiplying | Rinse and Repeat |

Now, I know what you're thinking. It seems impossible to create a successful e-commerce store and sell retail products while large retailers are announcing closures all over the world. But don't let that blind you to what's really happening!

Right now, everyone is purchasing online. In fact, consumers are more confident than ever to buy whatever they want through the internet. This is thanks to Amazon. Amazon has revolutionized the online retail industry, and retail sales overall! It has forever changed the way consumers buy products.

Amazon Revolutionized Retail

Yes, I am raving about Amazon. They have accomplished what no other company has in the history of retail. While many large retailers are suffering from the inevitable change in consumer purchasing behavior, Amazon has taken retailing to greater heights.

According to an article on investors.com, Ken Perkins, president of Amazon's Retail Metric, recently said, "I don't think many traditional retail CEOs would say publicly, 'Amazon is eating our lunch.'"

Over a decade ago, Amazon was just an online bookstore. That's it! Can you believe the biggest online retailer in the world got its start as a humble little platform for authors to self-publish their books online?

This is one way Amazon has affected retail for quite some time. Physical bookstores are now having a difficult time because people are geared toward buying books online. Next, Amazon expanded its operations to music and DVDs, and it saw an increase in sales simply by expanding its product line.

Today, of course, Amazon is a full e-commerce platform, selling everything - and I do mean everything - from pet accessories to watches to baby diapers and even groceries.

Most astonishing of all: **Amazon has now surpassed Walmart** in total revenue per year!

Yes, really!

As you may have read somewhere, Walmart generated over $482 billion in sales in 2015, but Amazon has now pummeled the big box retailer. It seems Amazon is serious about living up to its mission statement, which essentially says that it will be the utmost customer-centric company, where customers can buy anything they want online.

This is the very reason why Amazon invests an unprecedented amount into revolutionizing the way people buy: They have introduced Amazon Prime, AmazonFresh, and one-click Buy buttons. All of these have changed the way consumers spend their money, allowing them to use their credit card on a laptop, desktop, tablet, or mobile smartphone.

When I was a kid and the internet didn't exist, I would never have imagined people would put their credit cards through a computer, let alone a mobile phone. If you're like me, I bet you've had the same thought.

Not only that, but I bet there was a time, not long ago, when you weren't comfortable entering your credit card number on a computer.

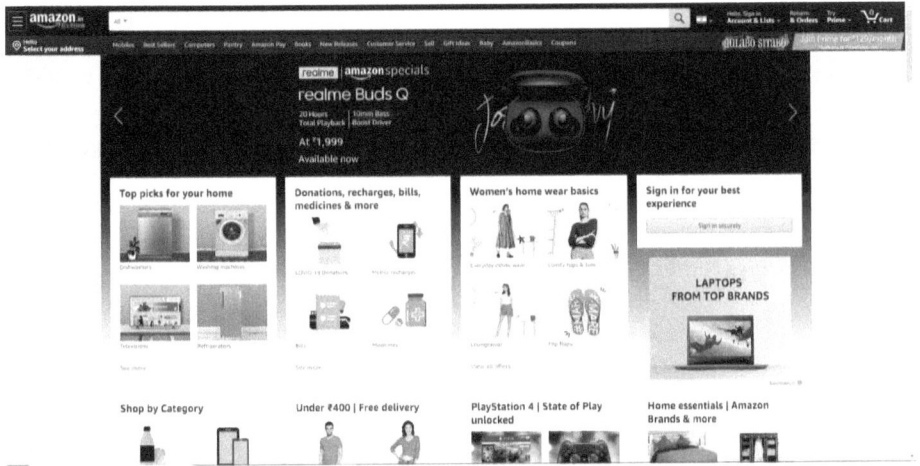

Guess what? Everything has changed! Online retail has evolved. People are now more than willing to spend money with their credit cards on a computer and even on a mobile phone.

You and I are not the only people who used to feel uncomfortable providing our credit card numbers online. Most consumers used to feel it was very unsafe to give away personal information. But because Amazon had such an incredible vision of what online retail could be, it was able to create a sea change in the retail industry by giving consumers the confidence to buy online.

This consumer confidence has allowed entrepreneurs like us, the average Joes, to ride the wave of Amazon's creation - the change that Amazon has spent a fortune to make. Online sales are so easy now, it is simply mind-boggling. We can create a website and start selling retail products online. Consumers are not afraid to purchase from us because they now understand that they have security. They can feel safe providing their personal information and entering their 16 credit card numbers on any website.

But Amazon has done so much more than simply putting the online consumer at ease. It has discovered the true magical formula to online retail success: Smart inventory!

Aside from all the innovative technology and infrastructure Amazon has built, there is one thing they do that has blown the traditional retail industry out of the water. I am willing to bet you aren't even aware of it. It has to do with how they structure their inventory - and it is this exact strategy that has helped me create Step 2 of my framework: Inventory arbitrage.

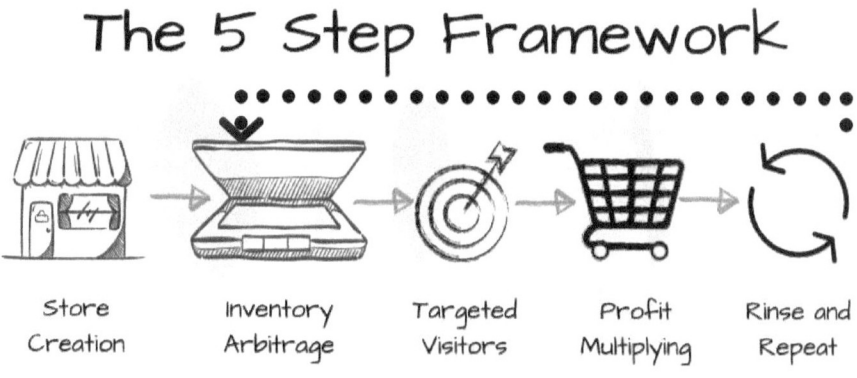

The 5 Step Framework

| Store Creation | Inventory Arbitrage | Targeted Visitors | Profit Multiplying | Rinse and Repeat |

It is this method of managing inventory that has made Amazon bulletproof, unlike other major retailers. This method is so simple it is almost beautiful in its simplicity. Ready for it?

Amazon doesn't actually own most of the inventory sold on its website.

Instead, Amazon has given the business of keeping inventory to the retailers. How clever is that? It has created a service called Fulfillment by Amazon that allows small to large enterprise retailers to hold inventory at their locations and fulfill the orders for all the other retailers.

So when it comes to keeping inventory, Amazon can wash its hands of the whole thing!

This is where the magic truly lies. I know a lot of people who have leveraged Amazon platforms and used Fulfillment by Amazon to build a seven-figure business, even if they had a small operation and worked from home. And this is just fine for Amazon.

Since everyone is putting their inventory on Amazon, it has allowed Amazon to list all these products on its website. Amazon makes a profit on every single transaction and builds its retail e-commerce business, and because it doesn't have to hold any inventory, it generates cash flow like nothing before.

Believe me, I know how insane that sounds. In Business 101, we learned that inventory is cash. Yet Amazon has been able to build an entire empire with barely any investment in inventory.

Using Walmart as an example, it has to invest millions of dollars in inventory just to open one store. That amount does not even include the cost of real estate or the cost of employees. It's a significant amount of money that Amazon doesn't need to lay out, which means Amazon can invest its cash in places where other brick-and-mortar retailers cannot.

When I learned about this method of doing retail business, I had my "Aha!" moment. This method of doing retail business led me to discover the concept inventory arbitrage. It allowed me to understand that manufacturers and vendors are more than happy to hold inventory for you while you simply focus on selling.

This is the exact strategy I am going to show you. I'm going to lay it all out for you. I will tell you who to work with and how to deal with vendors so that you can have your own e-commerce website just like Amazon, selling thousands or even tens of thousands of products without holding a single one in inventory.

Retail Is Still Profitable

I said it before, and I'll say it again: You can still make insane profits through retail, specifically through e-commerce. It may sound like a horror story when you hear about retailers shutting down globally and how there is tremendous change happening in the industry. But e-commerce is not only immune to this change; it is the driver of this change.

It's not hard to see why. Total retail sales in the United States in 2022 are projected to hit $6.03 trillion, up from $4.35 trillion in 2012. Yes, you heard that correctly. I said trillion, not billion. Retail sales in the U.S. alone will surpass the $6 trillion mark in 2022! In Europe, the numbers are equally impressive. In 2018, the European retail market value reached around 2.6 trillion euros. The estimated value for 2020 is set at 2.8 trillion euros. [3]

That's not chump change!

Regardless of what has happened in our economy over the past few years, people will still buy goods. People will still use their hard-earned money to buy the things they want.

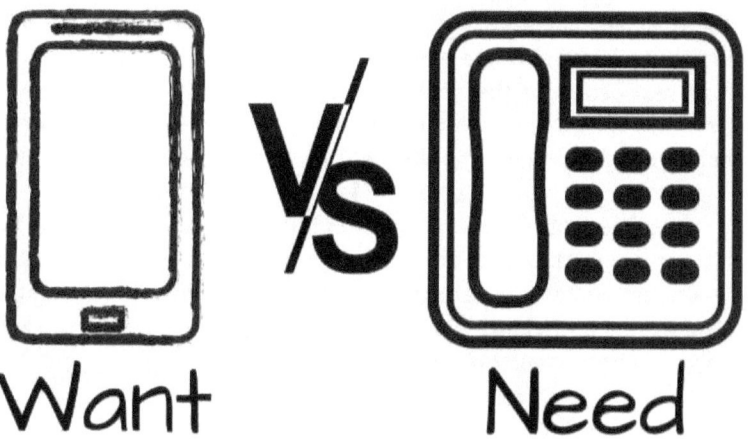

This is very important. I basically just said, "People buy whatever they want." Right now, your focus is to understand the first rule of buying behavior. The number one factor in a consumer buying an item is that they will buy based on their wants, not their needs.

You are not going to sell groceries or diapers because those things are based on need. When you sell based on need, you can never create a highly profitable business. You will be restricted by the cost of living, the amount of goods actually needed, and changes in the economy.

The bottom line is people buy based on their desires and their wants. Look at it this way. You need to buy a car because you need to get from point A to point B. But any old car will do, right? You could open up a newspaper right now and buy any old piece of junk for a couple hundred bucks. This car will fulfill your need because all you are trying to do is get from point A to point B.

But here's the thing...

People won't buy that piece of junk for a couple hundred bucks. Why? Because they don't want it. People buy based on wants. They want the nicest BMW. They want the nicest Mercedes. They want a Ferrari. All these luxury cars are based on wants.

Luxury brands are all based on wants.

Now, for all you women out there, I'm going to use another analogy. You need a purse, right? You need a purse in which to put your wallet. You need a purse in which to put your makeup. You need a purse in which to put your keys. But why don't you just use a plastic bag? Or maybe one of those reusable shopping bags? Why not use a fanny pack?

Because you don't want those things!

Why does everyone want a Louis Vuitton bag? Why does everyone want a Gucci? It's because people buy based on wants. This is how luxury brands are able to sell you a product that costs you thousands, but costs them less than $30 or $40 to make. Vuitton and Gucci can do this because they have created a want.

They *make* you want it!

As an e-commerce entrepreneur, your job is to find and sell products that people will buy based on their wants. The key is to buy these items for a low price and sell them at a high price. If you can find a low-supply product and a high-demand market, you are almost guaranteed to make insane profits right from the start.

Let's put this in a different way. Do you play games? Why? Because you like games and you want to play them. People don't need to play games. They want to play games.

The game Angry Birds is the perfect example. A company that took the simple concept of having birds catapulted through the air to kill pigs is now worth billions of dollars because people want to play the game. That's how companies are able to make a tremendous impact. It's how companies are able to profit. They sell products at a high cost while investing a low amount of money per unit.

Simple, right?

But you also absolutely have to understand another critical fact...

Although the multi-trillion dollar industry is very lucrative, many people will still fall into the trap of following the old-fashioned retail method, which poses a great threat of failure. If you follow the old retail method, you will either lose a lot of money or you will stress out like never before. At this point in history, there is a stress-free, modern method you can use to profit from retail. This method does not require any knowledge or experience - and you can have your business up and running in just a few weeks.

Get ready.

I'm about to share this modern retailing method with you. I want to be sure you fully understand this method so you do not fall into the old-fashioned method.

I want you to succeed!

The Old-Fashioned Retail Method VS. The Modern Method

Capital. It's the word new business owners fear the most. It's the first word that comes to mind when people are introduced to the idea of opening a retail business.

After all, to start a business you need a large amount of capital to invest in your triple net and your monthly lease. You have to invest in your inventory. You have to invest in your point of sale system. You have to invest in employees. You have to have a substantial amount of cash flow just to keep the business running on a day-to-day basis.

Let's break this down further.

Old Fashioned Retail Method

Find a Real estate Agent   Rent/Buy a store   Find a vendor   Get a Bank Loan   Hire workers   Advertise Products

In the old days, in order to start a business, you would first have to find a real estate agent. Then you would have to go out, find, and buy or rent a perfectly located retail space. Then you would have to invest in renovating and decorating your store. You would then have to start dealing with every single vendor for whom you wanted to carry products.

Once you had all this in place, you would then have to find the capital to invest in inventory. This basically meant walking into a bank and asking for a loan. Finally, you had to find your new team members by advertising.

Starting a retail business used to be a massive undertaking. The amount of risk involved was substantial because you were not guaranteed that you were going to have any profit the minute you opened up that retail store.

When you open a brick and mortar retail store, you are never guaranteed that people are going to walk through your doors, pick up the products you are selling, go to the cashier, and give you their money. There is just no guarantee. When you are following the old-fashioned retail method, you have to spend a ton of money just to prepare for your opening - all without knowing whether you will succeed.

And time is money. You will be spending an enormous amount of time getting your old-fashioned retail store off the ground. It will take you at least six months to a year to get started. So you aren't just risking money; you are also risking your time, which is really just more money out the window.

But the 21st century technological revolution has changed all that. There is a now a far more efficient and risk-free way to start a business. What I'm talking about isn't entirely new. I was actually inspired by Michael Masterson, author of *Ready, Fire, Aim*. The concept is based on learning to shoot, whether it's a gun or bow. When learning this skill, you are taught to get ready, aim, and then fire. Well, I'm here to tell you that's what the old-fashioned retail method was all about.

Now, because of advancing technology and the evolving market, all you have to do is get ready, by creating an e-commerce website. Then you can go ahead and fire! You just start selling right away! **Open the store and start selling.** You don't aim until after you start selling; you perfect your strategy later on.

This is how you keep your risk minimal. In fact, to get a website up and running so you can sell products using my inventory arbitrage method, you will need less than $100.

Did you hear that? You will need *less than $100* to get started!

You won't be investing hundreds of thousands of dollars, thousands, or even hundreds of dollars. The modern method revolves around technology. It revolves around inventory arbitrage.

You really can get a website up and running and start selling right away and then perfect the system later. Your website, as we all know by now, is going to be an e-commerce website. The perfection doesn't start until Step 4 in my 5-Step Framework. Throughout Steps 1 to 3, you basically just get ready and fire.

Get ready and fire. That's how you ride the wave and start generating sales in a very short period of time.

Now, you might be wondering, "Is e-commerce right for everyone? Is it right for me? Can I do this? Do I have the technology and the knowledge to create an e-commerce store and use the strategy ready, fire, aim?"

The answer is yes!

Next, I'm going to share with you how e-commerce is right for everyone and how it is especially right for you. All you have to do is follow my 5-Step System. You will have an e-commerce website up and running so you can start selling retail products in no time.

Why E-Commerce is Right for You

With this new ability to create a retail outlet literally at our fingertips, we are now in the age of e-commerce.

Even if you have heard the word e-commerce before reading this, you might still be wondering what it actually means. E-commerce originates from the concept of commerce, something that is by no means new. Commerce is simply a business interchange of goods across a distance. This interchange can be within the same country, or it can be between foreign countries.

So what's with the "e"? By adding the "e" in front of the word "commerce," we change the meaning to "electronic commerce." It means that the interchange, the sale of goods and services, is completed electronically via the internet.

"But it must be difficult to get an e-commerce site up and running," you say.

It certainly looks difficult because there are many aspects. First, you need to actually create a website. That sounds difficult all on its own, but then you need to acquire and manage an inventory. You must have knowledge and prior experience to actually create an e-commerce store, right?

Wrong! Absolutely Wrong!

I have one question for you at this point. Do you know how to use a computer? If the answer is yes, then you can start an e-commerce store. Thanks to today's technology, you don't need to have any prior knowledge or experience to create an e-commerce store.

But what about the advertising? How do you write ads that attract people? Fortunately, you don't even need to be a copy writer to start a successful e-commerce site.

Okay, it's true that when you create a business, you have to create ads and convey information about your products. You need to write sales material that will draw people in.

But here's the thing. Because of the evolving market, and because people are all about buying items online, you don't need to be a great copywriter. As long as you can write something informative, that's all that matters. All you have to do is describe the products you are selling and have them available in your store. That's it!

Copy writing is not something that you need to perfect when it comes to e-commerce.

Now, we have talked about why you don't need prior experience to open an e-commerce site, but there is another reason e-commerce can work for anyone and everyone. It has to do with overhead expenses. E-commerce is right for everyone because it keeps your costs low. As I mentioned earlier, right now the cost to start a business is at an all-time low. This is especially true of an e-commerce business.

Think about it. If you were to go the old-fashioned route, finding a physical retail location, stocking inventory, and hiring employees, your startup and operational costs would be through the roof. But with e-commerce you don't need any of that. You don't even need employees! You can be a work-at-home mom or dad and start creating an e-commerce store just like that!

The beauty of e-commerce is that you can work any time of the day. You can even *make money while you sleep* because e-commerce doesn't have the same limitations as brick-and-mortar commerce. Your website is open 24 hours a day, seven days a week. It doesn't matter if you don't have anyone working on the website or filling the orders 24 hours a day. You have access to the globe, which means that there will be consumers browsing your website and placing orders 24 hours a day.

Anyone, anywhere, anytime can go to your website to make a purchase.

This is the main difference between the old-fashioned retail method and the modern method. With today's technology powering e-commerce, your store is up and running 24/7, 365 days a year. It is even open during holidays. You simply cannot do that with an old-fashioned retail store. For that you have to have employees, you have to open the store at specific times, and you can't be open 24 hours a day because it costs too much. Your overhead expenses would be astronomical!

Do you see how different - and how easy - e-commerce is?

If you are still in doubt, please keep reading. I am going to prove to you in the pages of this book how e-commerce is right for everyone. Modern technology, combined with my discovery of inventory arbitrage, will allow you to have an e-commerce website up and running in a matter of weeks. Best of all, you don't need to invest a significant amount of money. All you need is some time to put it all in place and execute.

How small an investment is required?

If you have $100 then you are all set. You're about to learn how you can have an e-commerce website up and running for just $100. And your first e-commerce website can be filled with hundreds or even thousands of products in any niches or categories you want.

Of course, there are so many thousands of products out there that you could sell, but chances are you don't want to sell just anything. You need to tap into your own unique interests and passions. Ultimately, you should find a product category or niche about which you are passionate.

Let's face it. A lot of the time, people go into retail just for the money. They want money to buy the newest car or the biggest house. But at the end of the day, if you just focus on the money, then you're doing nothing but putting yourself back into a boring 9 to 5 job.

If, on the other hand, you create an e-commerce website which sells products that you absolutely love, then you'll love dedicating your time and energy to it. Every time you work on it, you are going to be excited and happy.

I hope you are pumped and ready to get started because I am now going to share with you everything you need to know to get it all off the ground. I will share information on how to deal with the technology and get the entire inventory; essentially everything you need to know to get an e-commerce store up and running. I'm going to share my step-by-step method on how to do this.

So, if you are still wondering whether e-commerce right for you, let me tell you this: If you take this book, read every single word in it, and actually apply the knowledge and execute the steps I share in these pages, you will find success. I can **guarantee** you e-commerce is right for anyone and everyone. We are in the **golden age of entrepreneurship** and technology.

Anyone - a twenty-year-old kid or even someone in high school - can start creating an e-commerce store right now.

There are absolutely no limitations here.

There are no restrictions.

And all you have to do is take action.

Chapter 3

The Digital Goldmine

The Multi Billion Dollar Industry

ARE YOU READY TO BE AMAZED?

We've already talked about the trillions of retail dollars being spent by consumers every year in the U.S. and around the world. But what about e-commerce?

E-commerce's percentage of these mind-boggling numbers keeps growing too. In fact, e-commerce sales more than doubled between 2010 and 2018. This phenomenal growth is expected to continue. In 2018[4] online sales of physical goods in the U.S. amounted to $504.6 billion and are projected to surpass $735 billion in 2023.[5] And because you'll be expanding globally, you might be interested to know some global e-commerce stats: In 2017, retail e-commerce sales worldwide amounted to $2.3 trillion and are projected to grow to $4.88 trillion in 2021.[6]

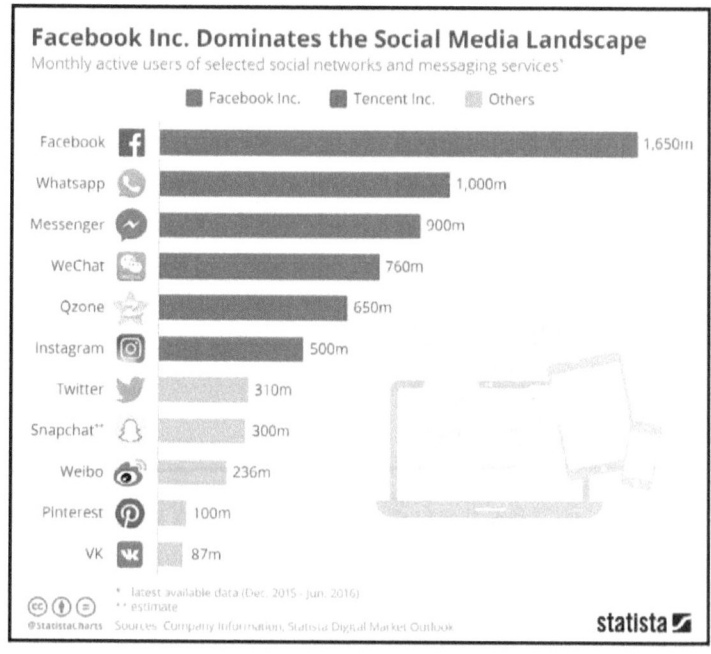

It is plain to see that we are in a period of exponential growth in the retail e-commerce industry.

With this in mind, I'm going to share with you the blueprint you need to follow so you can grab a piece of that multi-trillion dollar pie. After all, with that much money flowing through online retail businesses, there is plenty to go around! A small fraction of it can easily provide you with a seven-figure business empire.

[4]

Always remember that right now, we are at the beginning of this great journey. This is the rising age of e-commerce and there are many aspects [5] of e-commerce that are evolving, pushing e-commerce sales to even greater heights.

[6]

Perhaps one of the greatest aspects of the rise in e-commerce is the introduction and development of mobile technology. Mobile retail e-commerce sales are booming! Let me share a story with you to illustrate the rise - and power - of mobile e-commerce.

This is a story about how I turned a business around simply using mobile technology. Right now, we are in a mobile retail e-commerce era. Once again, Amazon is at the forefront of this change, having completely revolutionized how people make purchases through mobile phones.

When I started my e-commerce business, I was only focused on browser-based e-commerce, to be found on desktop and laptop computers. To my peril, I did not focus on mobile at all.
One day, it hit me. I was looking at the statistics and realized that mobile retail sales had been growing exponentially. This year alone, it is expected that the U.S. will see an astonishing $123 billion in mobile retail sales.

That's a **lot of money** on the table!

In fact, right now there are actually more mobile phones in use than laptops or desktops. Mobile phones and devices really open up a whole new world for everyone. People now have access to the internet right at their fingertips, no matter where they are. They are no longer tied to their home internet service.

They can be sitting in a coffee shop in London, touring the Eiffel Tower, on safari in Africa, or at a restaurant in their hometown.

What does all of this mean for those of us in the e-commerce business? What did it mean for me? It meant that there was a big piece of the pie that I wasn't capturing.

The moment I had this realization, I turned my business plan around and established my mobile e-commerce presence. I have invested a substantial amount of money to ensure that my website is what I call "mobile friendly" or "mobile responsive." This means that I have made sure that absolutely **every single mobile device** can see my website properly. My site will load fast and it has a very user-friendly interface, where people can find exactly what they want.

So, what happened?

Well, my investment was far from wasted. The day I launched my mobile e-commerce stores, my sales went through the roof! **My sales increased nearly 50%** in the first week - simply by turning my site into a mobile e-commerce store that allowed people with a mobile device to browse and make purchases.

It has been over seven months since my mobile e-commerce website was launched, and mobile now accounts for nearly 80% of our sales. Sales are well into eight figures right now - and 80% of that is a lot of money. And it is all because consumers' buying behavior has changed and I changed with it. Consumers now have the confidence to buy via mobile and that is where the opportunity starts.

But it doesn't end there, not by a long shot.

There is now another aspect of e-commerce that is blossoming and growing quickly: social commerce. Right now, there are many brands and many small businesses that utilize social media to build a brand presence, create sales, and gain traffic. Most important, social media is also a platform through which you can interact with your customers and your prospects. This means you can better understand your market and grow your business even further.

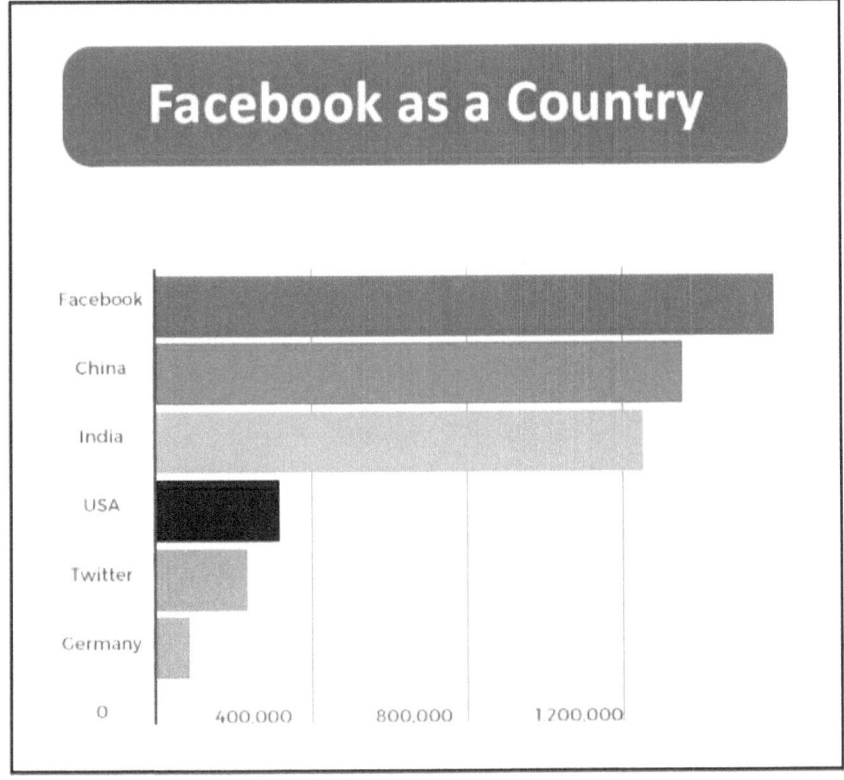

E-commerce in social media is something you cannot ignore. Take Facebook as a prime example. Facebook is the number one social media platform on the internet. It has over 2 billion users every single month. We are talking about the population of China and a few Germanies using Facebook every month. That is a lot of people!

Facebook is not alone.

The growing sector of social media marketing involves a number of other platforms. There are many people making money on Instagram, for example. They are creating a brand, showcasing their products, and sharing their product tips and information through Instagram. Since Instagram has now reached over 1 billion active users, these marketers have a wide audience.

Pinterest is another major force in the social media game. Right now, it has over 250 million monthly users. If you focus your strategy specifically on social commerce, I can guarantee you will have a business flooded with customers in a very short amount of time.

In fact, a business that is not based on your own passion will collapse in a very short time because you will not be committed to it over the long term. You won't want to waste your energy and time on it.

Believe me. Even if that business is generating a profit, you will gradually get bored with it and eventually you will not want to deal with it anymore.

In order for you to have a life-long, sustainable business, you need to find something you are absolutely passionate about - not just something random that you think will sell. That is where a lot of people fail. So many entrepreneurs and so many small businesses fail in the beginning because they try to enter a niche market in which they have absolutely no interest.

For example, if you like turtles, read about turtles, go scuba diving to swim with turtles, and have an overwhelming love of turtles, then that is your market. "Turtles" is your niche. You can create an entire e-commerce website all about turtles. It can include turtle accessories, turtle t-shirts, bracelets with turtles on them, toy stuffed animal turtles, and anything else related to turtles.

Your website can include all of that because right now, using inventory arbitrage, you have access to literally millions of products - and you can actually sell them. "Turtles" is a great example of a passion that you can use as a niche for an e-commerce store which revolves around turtle-related items. This level of passion is a very important key to success.

But what if you don't have an obvious passion, or you aren't sure if your passion would make a great e-commerce store?

Fortunately, Amazon can help! Remember, Amazon is the king of e-commerce, having made it what it is today. eBay is also a great source for passion niche research. If you need help narrowing down a niche market, simply go to Amazon.com or eBay.com, and look at their top categories.

You'll instantly find hundreds of categories to consider. Think about Home and Gardening.

Are you a person who loves your home environment, someone who loves gardening, cooking, and home décor? If that's the case, then the Home and Gardening niche would be perfect for you.

If not, maybe you are a person who loves camping, hiking, and outdoor activities. If that is what you are passionate about, then you can choose the outdoor gear/camping gear niche.

The main thing is that you choose something you love.

Now, choosing a niche will be easy for some, but for others it can be very difficult. Some people even feel so discouraged about not discovering their niche that they abandon the idea of building an e-commerce store. Don't do this!

Instead, answer this question: What is the first thing that comes to mind when I ask you, "What are you passionate about?" The answer that immediately pops into your mind is your intuition at work. This is your subconscious telling you what you absolutely love. Follow that thought! Follow that intuition - and go after that market!

Most of all, do not allow anything deter you or get in your way. Don't let your loved ones, your partner, your children, or your friends and family tell you what you should or shouldn't do. Your first intuition is always going to be the best. It will be the idea you never regret. Go with that idea. Go with that market. And start taking action.

As I said earlier, you are entering a unique environment in which you get ready, fire, and then aim. In other words, you will perfect the process - including the products you sell - after you start selling.

Right now, follow your intuition. I promise you it is the right thing to do because I have seen many people, including my students, waste a lot of time trying to define their perfect niche.

Don't waste time this way. Finding your niche is very simple. It is simply what you are absolutely passionate about.

There's one last thing you need to know before we continue.

When you begin creating your e-commerce store, I recommend that you don't attempt a multi-departmental site. At this point, there's no need to be the next Walmart, selling everything from clothing to TVs to electronics to groceries. That's too big - at least in the beginning.

Instead, focus on one specific market - a very narrow market. This lets you get your feet wet while minimizing your risk. This works greatly to your advantage. Later in this book, I'm going to share with you how to use social commerce to fine tune your business and find your hungry buyers. Once you have mastered the first four steps of the Five-Step System, you will rinse and repeat by creating a larger e-commerce outlet. This is when you can add more departments to your e-commerce site.

However, no matter where you are in your e-commerce journey, I still favor niche stores. My reasoning is simple. A niche store allows you to develop a relationship with your customer. Every person who buys from you is a real person. When you have a niche store, you know what that person's interest is and this information is crucial when you're scaling up your business. I explain this in more depth later in this book. For now, all I want you to remember is that your customers will spend more money to buy more from you if you establish a relationship with them.

But we are getting ahead of ourselves. Right now, I want you to write down on a piece of paper the niche you are pursuing.

Go on. Write it down.

Congratulations!

What you have just written is going to be your first e-commerce store.

Secure a Domain

You now know the niche market you're targeting with your e-commerce store. This makes it possible for you to secure your web address. With a physical brick and mortar location, you have a physical address: the street name, postal code, state/province, and country.

In the online world, you have a similar way to identify yourself: a web address. Your web address is simply your domain, www.TheName.com, .co, .net, .io, or your country's extension, such as .ca for Canada. That's all there is to it. This is your web address. This is the address that people type into their browser to visit your online retail store.

It is important to understand that your domain is an important part of your brand image. You want to find a name that fits your niche. If you have chosen a panda niche, then your domain name should be something related to pandas.

However, you can't use a domain name that someone else is already using.

To find out whether a domain name is already taken, simply go to www.GoDaddy.com or www.NameCheap.com. There are many other domain name services out there, but I personally prefer GoDaddy.com.

There you will find a very large search field on the home page. Simply type in the domain name you want and it will instantly state whether the domain is available

Keep in mind that you cannot have underscores or spaces between the words in your domain name. You can use hyphens, but I strongly suggest you look for words that can be tied together.

When you enter your domain name in the GoDaddy search box, you will find similar domains that are secured by other businesses. But you want to be unique. You want your domain name to stand out and not be easily confused with that of another business.

Your best bet is to choose a domain name with two to three words in it. When you type it in, GoDaddy will tell you if someone owns that domain or not. At times, you will see something called a premium domain. Avoid this at all costs!

Please, do not fall into the trap of purchasing a premium domain. You are in the very early stages of creating your brand. You don't need to spend thousands or tens of thousands of dollars on a web address. Seriously, that's what these premium domains cost. Go with something that is available and that is at market price, which is a mere $10 a year.

Take the time to research your options.

I often use Source.com or Dictionary.com to look for potential domain name words. All you have to do when you find something that is available is purchase it. It will only cost you $9.99 or so for one year. Obviously, the pricing may be slightly different. Sometimes you can get a domain for cheaper than that!

Now, as you go through the process of purchasing your domain name on GoDaddy or NameCheap, you will be asked if you want to add items like privacy for your domain info, an email address for your domain, and a web hosting server.

All of that can be ignored.

All I need you to do right now is secure your name and spend the $10. Out of the $100 that we have allocated to getting your e-commerce store off the ground, you just spent $10. Now you are left with $90 to get your e-commerce store ready to go.

Have you done it yet? Have you secured your domain name?

If you haven't, then do it now. It's very simple. Once you have your market niche and you know what you want to go after, purchase a domain. Secure it and it will become your brand.

Once you have secured your domain, I'm going to show you how you can start creating your brand presence without any knowledge or experience. You don't need to be a designer to create your brand. In the final installment of this chapter, I am going to share exactly how to create your brand.

Creating your Brand Presence

You did it! I know you did!

Now that you have secured your domain name, your next immediate task is to create a logo. Now, I want to be clear on this from the start: You do not need the perfect be-all and end-all logo right now. Do not get lost in the process of creating your logo. Do you need something nice looking and eye-catching? Sure, but you don't need to perfect it. Not yet.

Many businesses, including Google, Microsoft, and Yahoo, change their logo from time to time. Coca-Cola is a great example. The company has changed its logo several times over the many decades it has been in business.

Keep that in mind. You really don't need to come up with a logo right now that will stick with your brand for life. Having said that, you still need something off the top, a logo that will help you create your brand and give your brand a presence on the internet.

There are two different ways for you to create your logo without being a designer and without knowing how to use a design program. The first way is go to www.Fotolia.com. Fotolia.com is an image website that is owned by Adobe.

When you go to the site, you will have access to an immense library of pictures and logos. Choose an image or logo you want to use, pay a very small price, and you will have the right to use that image as your logo.

To search their huge library of images, go to Fotolia.com. You will see a search field on the homepage. In this search field, simply type the keyword of your domain name or the name of your niche.

Let's use "Dogs" as our niche. The "Dogs" brand is what we are going to create together.

Ready?

Type in the keyword "Dogs" plus the word "logo." (Use your own keyword plus "logo" if you prefer.) When you hit Search, a multitude of different images of possible turtle logos will instantly appear. You'll see many graphic designs and logos from which to choose. All you have to do is click the one you want and purchase the image. Now you can use it for your e-commerce store and for all related material in the future.

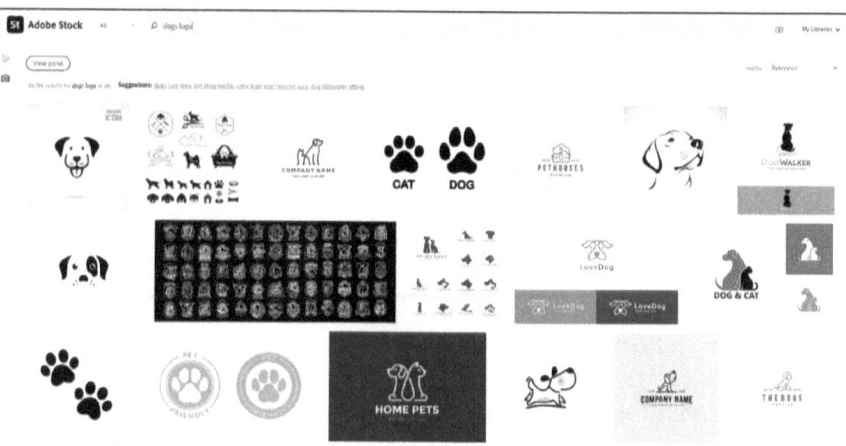

But what if Fotolia.com doesn't have an image or logo you like? What if nothing catches your eye? You still need a logo, but you want a logo that you love. Fortunately, there is another option. You can outsource!

Outsourcing is basically hiring a freelancer, an individual who can do the work for you. But don't panic! I'm not saying you need to spend thousands of dollars, or even hundreds of dollars to have your logo created by someone. In fact, it is incredibly inexpensive to have this done. All you need to spend is $5!

Yes, you read that correctly. You can stop rubbing your eyes now.

You can have your logo designed by a freelancer for a mere $5. You might be asking, "Where can I get a logo created for such a low price?"

Let me introduce you to <u>Fiverr.com</u>, where freelancers sell their expertise for a starting price of just $5. All you have to do is spend $5 to have your logo created.

When you visit <u>Fiverr.com</u>, go to "Graphic Design" and look for "Logo Design." There are many services that you can outsource on Fiverr: graphic design, digital marketing, writing and translation, video and animation, and music and audio services. At this point in your journey, you are using Fiverr specifically to create your logo.

In the Logo Design category, the freelancers are automatically listed from highest average customer review to lowest. I suggest you choose someone based on their previous customer recommendations. Click on a profile and look at the work portfolio to see what they do. Be sure to check the client feedback and ratings to ensure that other people were happy with this freelancer's service. Otherwise, you just won't know what you are getting into.

What is a good rating? Anything over a 4.5-star rating is ideal. The closer to a 5/5 or 100% rating, the better. These are the people you want to work with. You might look through someone's individual ratings and feedback and see an odd one that isn't great. That doesn't mean anything. Obviously, as we all know, people make mistakes and sometimes clients leave negative feedback. My benchmark is always a service provider who has a 90% rating (4.5/5) or above.If you stick with this rating level, you will get high quality work.

Fiverr is very straightforward. All you have to do is find the designer you want, proceed with the order, and provide the information requested.

Be sure to provide as much detail as you can in terms of what you envision for your logo, including preferred colors, style, and what your e-commerce website sells including preferred colors, style, and what your e-commerce website sells. The more details you give designers, the easier it is for them to create something you love. Once you have placed your order, sit back and let the designer do the work.

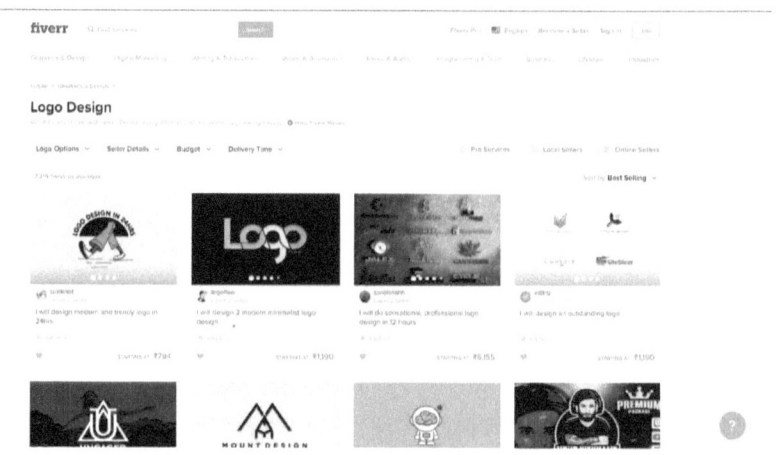

Now, if the design you get needs a change, some graphic designers will provide revisions in their price - while others may not. The freelancer's profile should clearly show his or her revision policy. Overall though, it only costs $5 to have a premium logo created. That's a great deal!

So, let's check your status. Where are we in the creation of your e-commerce store?

You have purchased your domain and you have used Fiverr to create your logo. This means that at this point you have spent $15 of your $100 budget. Fabulous!

If your logo isn't created yet, go to Fotolia.com or Fiverr.com now and do it. You need to execute.

You chose your market, you secured your domain, and now it's time to create your logo.

Now is the time to execute.

Chapter 4

The Wizard of E-Commerce

Technology can turn you into an
E-Commerce Giant

How easy is it to create an e-commerce website?

Well, do you know how to turn on a computer? Can you go online? Do you know how to use Microsoft Word?

I can virtually guarantee you that if you can do these things, then you can create your own e-commerce website. Really! Thanks to the innovations in our industry, you no longer need to pay thousands or even hundreds of dollars to create an e-commerce store with full functionality.

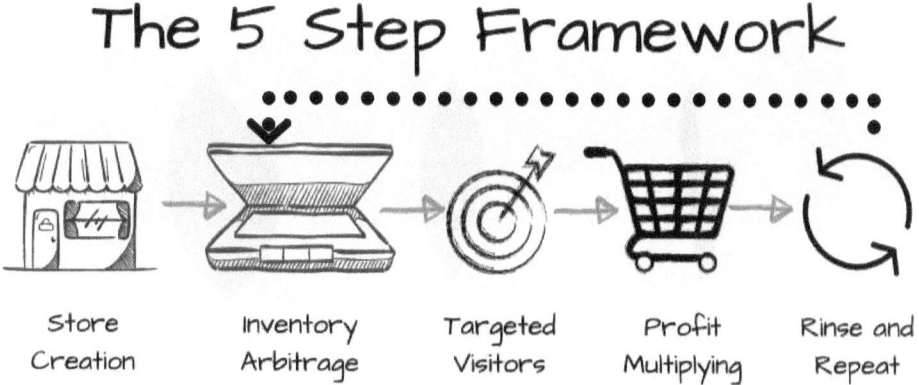

The 5 Step Framework

Store Creation • Inventory Arbitrage • Targeted Visitors • Profit Multiplying • Rinse and Repeat

You don't need a lot of money nor do you need to be tech savvy or experienced. As long as you know how to copy, paste, and type out the words you would like to appear on your website, voilà! Everything is done.

Want to know the best part?

Even though you aren't paying big bucks to hire help, you can still be guided through the process. There are so many online training videos that you can simply go to YouTube and learn how to create your site.

The majority of these YouTubers are e-commerce store owners in their own right, so they know what they're talking about. Many of them also have something extra that I love: live chat support that allows them to personally guide you through the entire website creation process.

There is absolutely zero excuse for you not to create your own website that sells physical or digital products online.

This may feel a bit overwhelming and you may be thinking, "Wow! I need to create a website with full functionality." But if you follow the steps I give you here, you can have a website up and running in no time.

In the current marketplace, there are many e-commerce website creation companies from which you can choose. These include Volusion, PrestaShop, Magento, BigCommerce, Infusionsoft, and 1ShoppingCart. Each of these is classified as an industry giant. However, with these platforms, you still need to have a basic understanding of how to program a website. In fact, you need to know how to synchronize everything and put it online.

Fortunately, you have two other options which really will make your life easier. These two current industry drivers allow any newbie to create their own online e-commerce website: WooCommerce and Shopify.

Before we talk about the advantages and disadvantages of WooCommerce and Shopify and why you should choose one over the other, please know this…

Right now we are in a golden era of retailing. You don't need to worry about programming and you don't have to worry about design. These can be done easily and I'm going to guide you through the entire process.

Comparing The Two Industry-Leading Technologies

So, what about these two amazing, industry-leading technologies, WooCommerce and Shopify? Is one better than the other? Well, this is my personal opinion, but after many years of experience I recommend Shopify over WooCommerce.

Having said that, you can't make a decision if you don't have all the facts. So I'm going to share with you information about both of these platforms. From there, you can make your final decision.

Let's talk about WooCommerce first. WooCommerce is WordPress-based. Now, we have all heard of WordPress. It's that blogging platform, right?

Well, WordPress isn't just for blogging anymore. In fact, WordPress is known to be the best CMS (Content Management System) for any beginner who is creating a website. The user interface is very easy to use - and that's not even the best part.

The best part is that WooCommerce is absolutely free to use!

There are no monthly fees or any other hidden fees. All you pay for is your website hosting service, and you are all set. However, I have found that the one major flaw with WooCommerce and WordPress in general lies in their security or lack thereof.

WooCommerce is built on top of WordPress and WordPress is a very vulnerable platform. WordPress is a target for many hackers. Even a novice hacker can breach WordPress sites with relative ease. There is also a massive amount of customer information on WordPress servers! If you use WooCommerce, it will leave you and your business very vulnerable unless you invest in your own security to prevent such security breaches. I know I would not be able to sleep at night knowing my customer information wasn't secure.

"No problem," you think, "I can invest in security software."

Unfortunately, this will cost you a substantial amount of money every month, which is a huge investment - a lot more than the $100 we're staying under.

Please understand that I am not giving you third-hand information about WooCommerce and WordPress. I personally experienced a horror story that shows what can happen with WordPress.

When I first launched my startup, I got into serious trouble with WordPress. Right smack in the middle of a campaign that was generating a bucket-load of traffic, I got hacked. My partners and I discovered that this hack affected the up-time of our site.

The hackers didn't steal any information from our website. Instead, they stole my business! They installed specific codes on my site by hacking into WordPress, accessing my site, and changing my product links. When customers went to purchase one of my products, they were redirected to a completely different website that I did not own!

I still remember it clearly. The hacker was trying to make affiliate commissions by redirecting my traffic to a site that gave a different offer. They even went as far as demanding a ransom for the site to be restored. I want you to consider how scary this was - along with the potential for total disaster to my business. If you have WooCommerce with your WordPress account, you have a lot of customer information there - including credit card information.

This lack of security will leave you liable to your customers and to the public. Why? Because hackers can go in and steal all of your customer information and use it for illegal purposes.

Do you want that liability? Do you want that level of worry?

This leaves us with the second option, Shopify. It is one of the main reasons why I choose Shopify over WooCommerce. I have to say that moving to Shopify was the best move I ever made for all of my businesses - especially my online e-commerce stores.

Shopify is amazing!

For one thing, it has one of the best mobile e-commerce checkout pages I've ever seen. I have already discussed the massive power of mobile e-commerce. If your website and your checkout process are not mobile responsive, you are leaving a lot of money on the table.

Can you guess how much of a drastic change my business experienced when I changed into Shopify? Here's my Shopify story.

Before I switched to Shopify, My businesses including my e-commerce stores were using another third party cart software. Now, don't get me wrong. The online shopping cart is a pioneering achievement for e-commerce providers and I had mastered its use. I was, however, spending a lot of money each month with them for all my accounts.

Then I discovered one major problem as I was looking at my website analytics. I was losing out on mobile sales, big time! Out of my entire annual sales, only 10% was coming from mobile devices.

I knew I had to make a drastic change in the way I operated my business. If I didn't change with the times, my business would eventually collapse. The first move I made was to check out Shopify. Lo and behold, I saw that a lot of major companies use Shopify as their platform. The main reason is because of Shopify's enhanced mobile checkout platform.

I wasted no time making the change. I literally transferred my business to Shopify overnight. Within one week, my sales took a 180° turn. Now, every one of my e-commerce stores brings in over 80% of sales straight from mobile. My overall annual sales have increased dramatically, because now I'm able to scale my businesses within the mobile industries.

With Shopify, you have access to hundreds of apps that allow you to create and enhance your online store for outstanding customer interaction.

Now, I am well aware that nothing is perfect. Shopify is no exception.

There is one disadvantage Shopify as compared to WooCommerce: a small monthly fee. The pricing starts at $29 a month. However, you don't need to pay a hosting fee on top of that. That saves a little bit of money.

Shopify costs more money than WooCommerce, because each month you pay at least $20 more than you would pay a hosting provider. You can find hosting providers for less than ten dollars a month right now when using WooCommerce, but with Shopify you have to pay $29.

But make no mistake...

I can virtually guarantee that *this $29 will be the best investment you make for your e-commerce store*. That being said, the best part about Shopify is that you can have as many different e-commerce stores as you want right at your fingertips. All you have to do is click a few buttons and you have an entire e-commerce site built.

Now, there are two other disadvantages to using Shopify. The first is their currency, and the second is the ability to create additional pages outside the store.

Let's talk about currency, first. If you are in the United States, then you will have absolutely no problem with this. However, if you are an international business owner, let's say from India, UK, Australia, or Canada, you are going to be restricted because of Shopify payment. I'll share more details about this in a later section.

What you need to know now, though, is that your default currency will not be in U.S. dollars. This may be a problem for you because it is very important that your online store accepts payment in U.S. currency, the number one trading currency in the world.

If you live outside the U.S., you have to use local currency when accepting payments. This will cause you to lose money due to the exchange rate.

Fortunately, there are apps you can purchase in Shopify that will allow you to get past this issue. For those of you who don't want to make that very small investment, currency will be a disadvantage.

The second disadvantage to Shopify is the need to create additional landing pages. A landing page is the page that people "land on" and visit to see what is available at your store. If they find what they like on the landing page, they will go through the buying process.

Now, this disadvantage applies mainly to advanced users. Creating an HTML or CSS landing page in Shopify is tedious. In fact, it is a downright complicated process just to have these types of landing pages on Shopify.

You can avoid this issue by creating pages through Shopify. This is a good solution for now, but you will be limited to Shopify's themes, structures, and infrastructure. There are other providers and apps out there that help you create landing pages, including Zero Up™ Lab. (This incurs an additional fee, outside of the $100 budget that we are talking about in this book.)

That said, it is still clear to me that Shopify is the superior choice when it comes to setting up your e-commerce store. For this reason, I have devoted the next section to showing you step-by-step how to get your Shopify store up and running, and how to configure it so you are ready to sell products.

Shopify Tutorial

Shopify is massive.

Shopify is the only publicly-traded e-commerce provider. At the time of this writing, it is trading at $189 a share. This means that Shopify must ensure that it delivers the best product in the industry so that it continues to draw a high demand for its product.

This is another major reason I choose Shopify over other e-commerce platforms; it's accountable not only to its customers but to its shareholders.

In this section I'm going to walk you step-by-step through the Shopify store setup and configuration process. I will show you how to have everything in place so that you can start putting up products and start selling.

What comes first?

Go to www.Shopify.com. Click the button that says **Start free trial.** At this
point, you'll enter your email address, create your password, and input
your store name - the niche or the domain name you chose earlier.

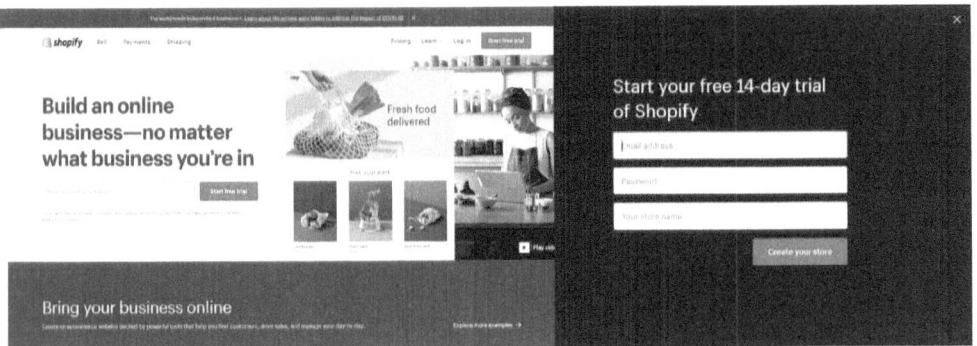

Now, Shopify offers a 14-day free trial period, but the free trial is not for
us. We are looking at this from a long-term perspective. So once you have
filled out all the information and created your account, I would like you to
upgrade your account to Basic Shopify, which you can select from the
pricing plans.

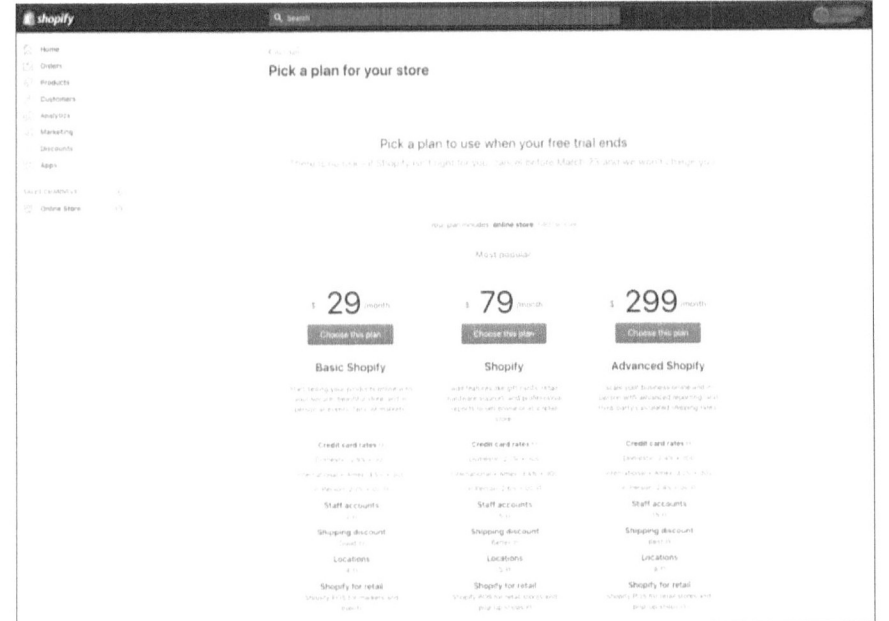

Basic Shopify will give you everything you need. At this point there is no need to upgrade to $79 or $299. You can leave that for when you start scaling your business. That's when you will start moving up the ladder.

For now, our sole purpose is to get your e-commerce store up and running to start generating sales.

Basic Shopify costs $29 a month.

Let's take a look at what we have spent so far: $10 on a domain, $5 on a logo, and now $29 on Basic Shopify. So, at this point in the journey to set up your e-commerce store, you have spent $44 of the $100 we talked about previously.

Once you upgrade to Basic Shopify, you are now ready to build your online store. Keep in mind that Shopify is not restricted to only online e-commerce stores. You can sell on Facebook, mobile app, even as a point of sale (POS) system. Many small brick and mortar businesses use Shopify's POS to take payments using a tablet. This is smart because it means they don't need to invest thousands of dollars for a physical POS; they can just use Shopify! For our purposes, we need Shopify's e-commerce retailing.

Now that you have activated your online store, click on **Online Store** from the side menu, then click on **Preferences from the drop-down**. Now enter your homepage title, which is the brand name you chose previously. Under the homepage meta description, provide a short description of what your store is about. This is for SEO-purposes so that your website can be indexed properly on the search engine results page, and the description will display just under your page link.

Next, scroll further down the page to the **Password Page section**. Uncheck the box next to "Enable password page" so that you are not blocking access to your store. Then simply click on **Save**.

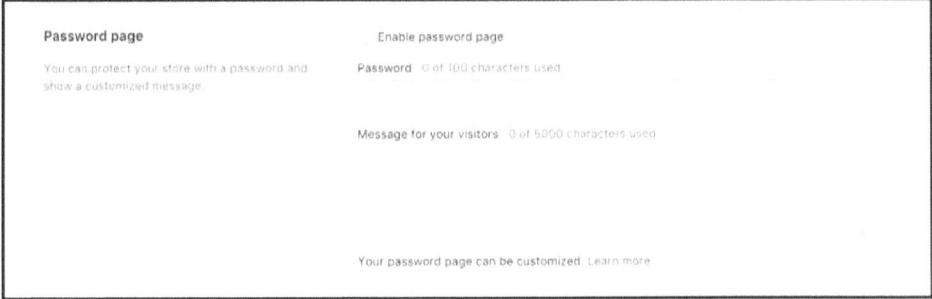

The next thing you need to do is go to **Domains**. You can find it under the Online Store sub-menu. Once you are there, click on **"Connect existing domain"** at the top. Then input the URL of the domain you just purchased, www.yourdomainname.com, and then click **Next**.

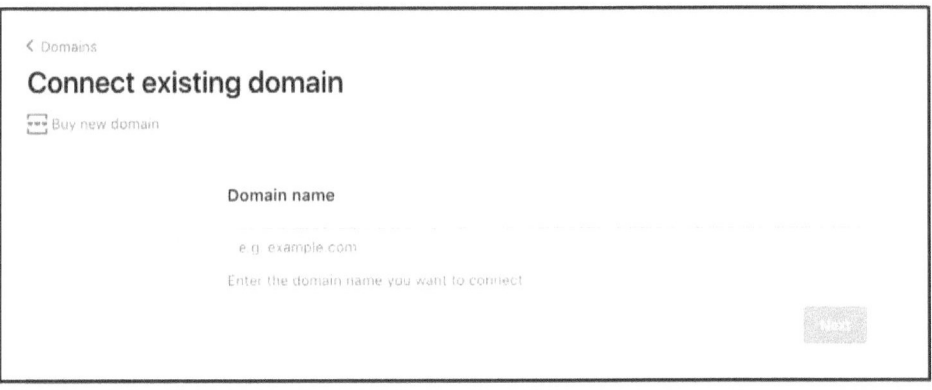

Once you have added your domain, Shopify will provide a step-by-step guide that will teach you how to have your domain attached to your store. I'm not going to go into this in depth here because Shopify covers it.

When you have your domain all set up, you need to go back to the main list on the left-hand side of the screen, click **Settings**, and then click **General**. This is where you configure the settings you will need for your store. Simply enter the information that you need to include. In the **Standards and formats** section you should put the time zone that you prefer and keep the metrics as is. Don't change the metrics.

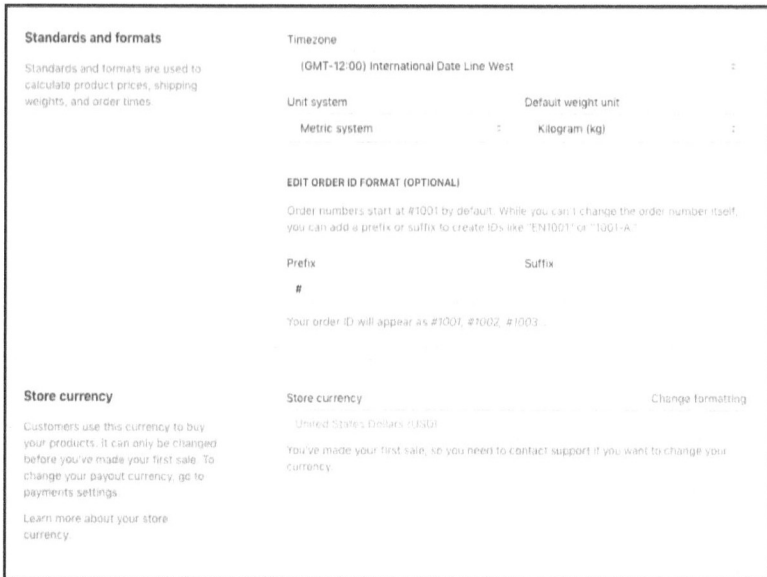

Next, while still in **Settings**, you will click on **Checkout**. The Checkout section is incredibly important! Under **Customer Accounts**, make sure **Accounts are disabled** is checked. You are doing this because you want the customer to check out as a guest. You don't want to make the entire buying process more complicated than it needs to be. People just want to buy! They don't want to create an account, so make sure that accounts are disabled!

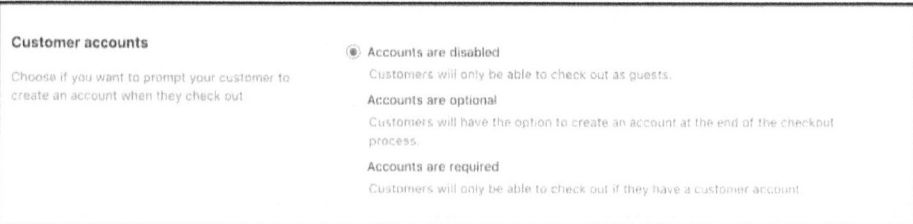

Next, in the **Form options** section, make sure that Require **last name only** is checked. Then ensure that **Company name** is checked as **Hidden**, and **Address line 2** is checked as **Optional**. There are people who have extremely long addresses, so you want to make it an option only.

You can choose whether or not to check **Shipping address phone number,** but I suggest hiding it in the beginning. As your company grows, you can change this to **Optional**; it will give you another way to get in touch with your customers.

Form options

Choose whether your checkout form requires
extra information from your customer

Full name

(●) Require last name only

Require first and last name

Company name

(●) Hidden

Optional

Required

Address line 2 (apartment, unit, etc.)

Hidden

(●) Optional

Required

Shipping address phone number

(●) Hidden

Optional

Required

Why are we hiding some fields, but not others?

When checking out, the more information people have to enter, the lower
your conversion rate will be. In other words, if people have to fill out a lot
of information, there is a greater chance they will just leave your checkout
before buying a thing. You don't want this to happen! This is why you
need to hide some of the fields in this form.

Next, you will go down to **Order processing** and make sure that both **Use
the billing address as the shipping address by default** and **Enable
address auto-completion are checked.** This is another way to reduce the
number of fields customers are required to complete in the checkout so
your new customers aren't overwhelmed.

Order processing

Change how your store responds to
checkout and order events. Learn
about order processing

While the customer is checking out

✓ Use the shipping address as the billing address by default

  Reduces the number of fields required to check out. The billing address can still be
  edited.

✓ Enable address autocompletion

  Gives customers address suggestions when they enter their shipping and billing
  address.

The next thing you need to do is ask permission! Yes, you will ask for your customers' consent to send promotional emails to them. Make sure you have both **Show a sign-up at checkout** and **Preselect the sign-up option** checked.

Now, I want you to understand that giving your customers the option to receive promotional material is very important, especially when you get to Step 4 of my 5-Step Framework. You absolutely must provide this email option. Here's what it looks like:

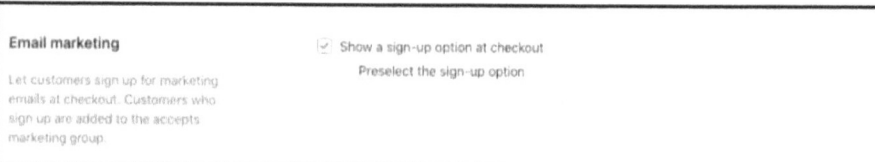

Then, press the **Save** button and you're all set here.

Next, you need to get your Legal pages in place. To do so, head over to the **Settings** tab on the bottom-right corner menu, then click on the **Legal** link. In this section, you'll be able to create your Refund Policy, Privacy Policy, Terms of Service, and Shipping Policy.

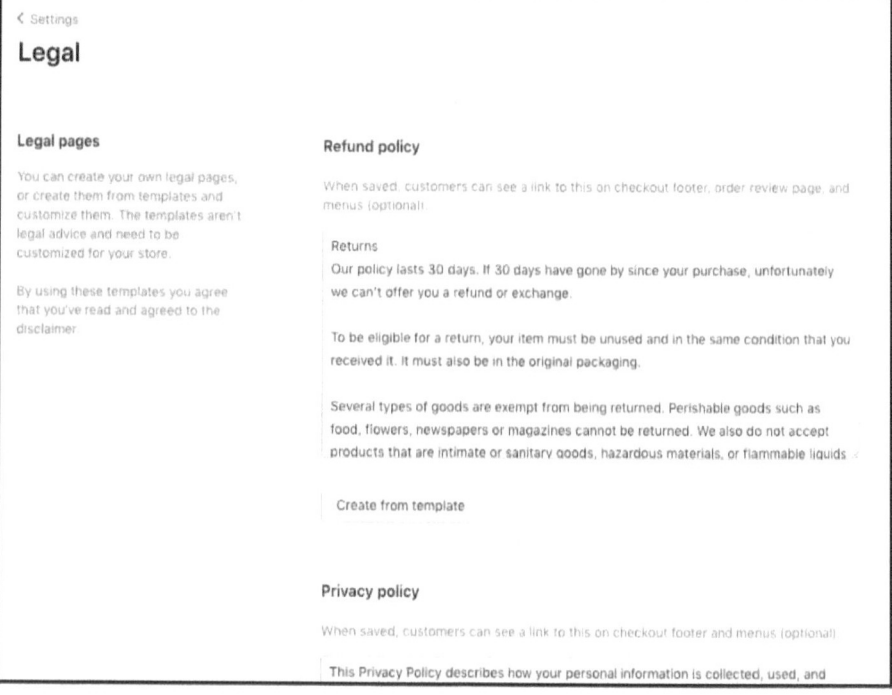

This is yet another advantage to using Shopify: You don't need to hire a lawyer to draft your refund policy, your privacy statement, your terms of service, or your shipping policy. The beauty of this platform is that it's all covered! All you have to do is click on the button that says **Generate sample refund policy**, and voilà! Your refund policy is automatically created. The same goes for your privacy policy, your terms of service and your shipping policy.

At this point, there is a little work involved. You should do your due diligence, read over the policies that are automatically generated, and make the necessary changes to ensure it is right for your e-commerce business. It's likely that you won't need to make any changes, but read it through so you have a basic understanding of these policies. Every website needs a refund policy, privacy policy, terms of service, and shipping policy because it is a legal entity; you are creating a legitimate business. These are very important pages to have on your website.

The final setup process is **Taxes**. I would love to help and give you my input, but I do not have the background to do so. I am not a legal consultant nor am I a tax consultant. Because I cannot give you the right answers or provide my feedback on this, you need to contact a local tax consultant or legal consultant to set the correct taxes for your store.

Now you get to have some fun! Go back under the **Sales Channel**, click **Online Store**, click Themes, and then click **Visit Theme Store.**

Shopify Theme Store
Browse free and selected paid themes using search and filter tools.

Visit Theme Store

In Shopify, developers have already created what we call a done-for-you website, so you can simply choose the theme you want and actually start creating your store. There are some premium themes for which you have to pay, but I suggest you avoid these for now. At the top of the screen, click on "All Themes", then filter your search by price to look at Free themes only.

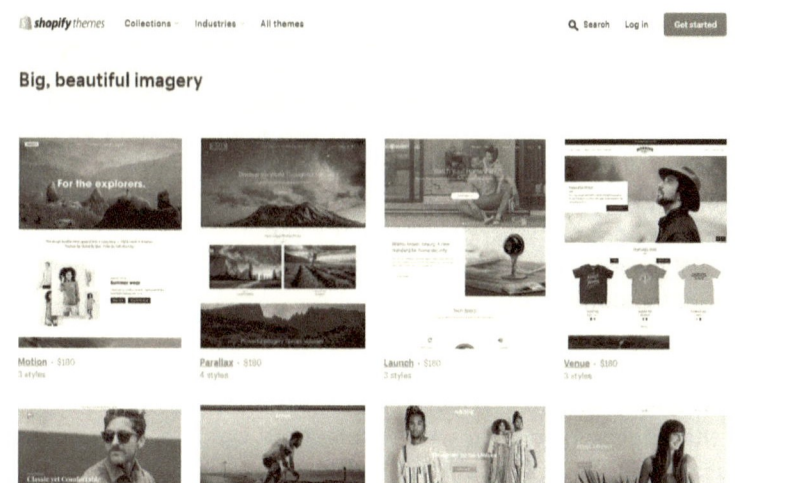

Big, beautiful imagery

There is really no point in spending money on a premium theme at this stage of the game. A free theme will be good enough and will do the job nicely. Under free themes, you can select whatever theme you like. There is a great selection from which to choose, so you are bound to find something you like. I love to keep my stores simple, so I will choose either the Parallax theme as that is a top used themes in Shopify. Of course, it is up to you to decide what theme you want.

Once you have clicked on the theme and installed it, you get to customize it!

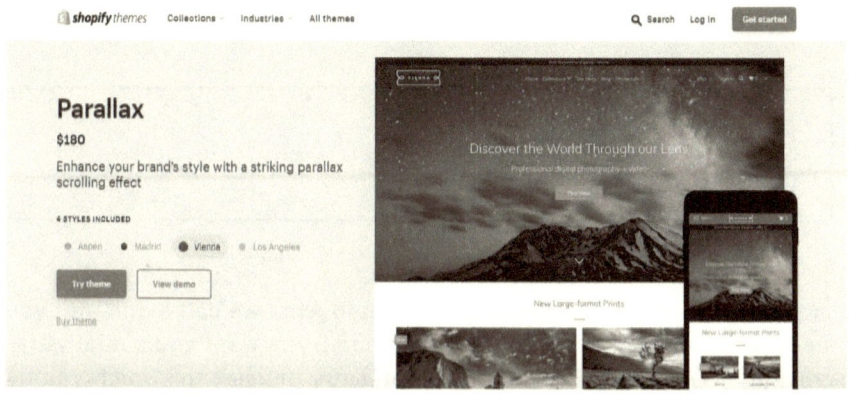

I love this part. It is not difficult to customize a theme. Once you click on **Customize Theme or Try Theme**, you will be brought into what we call what-you-see-is-what-you-get software.

You will see a list of pre-sets on the left-hand side of the screen that includes:

• Colors
• Typography
• Borders
• Header and navigation
• Footer
• Homepage
• Product Page
• Collection Page
• Cart Page
• Social Media
• Checkout

Just go into each of these sections, one at a time, and change the things that you would like to change. That's it! There is nothing difficult. No technical magic involved.

Now, remember that everything you do simply requires copy, paste, and typing. You don't have to know how to write code or program because everything is already done for you. All you have to do is click a few buttons, change the colors, upload an image, and that's it!

When it comes to images, be extremely careful. Do NOT go to www.google.com and search for any old image and use it. Why not? Because images can be copyrighted and you might infringe on another person's copyright. You can go to www.fotolia.com and buy royalty images.

But there is an even better option!

There is another website from which you can get royalty-free images - and you don't even need to include an attribution credit to the creator of that image. This website is www.pixabay.com. On pixabay.com you can simply type in keywords of the images you want, then copy and paste. You can use these images for your store.

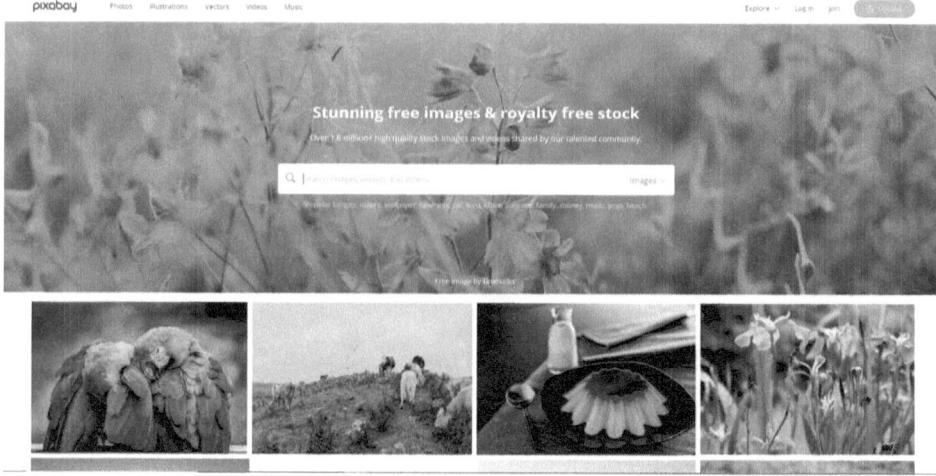

Now that you understand the basics of customizing your theme, changing the color, creating the brand, and uploading images, the next step is to add pages.

There are several pages that are incredibly important to have in your Shopify store. The first of these is an **About Us** page. If you go back into Shopify, you can click on **Online Store** and then click on **Pages**. In the top right-hand corner, click on **Add page**.

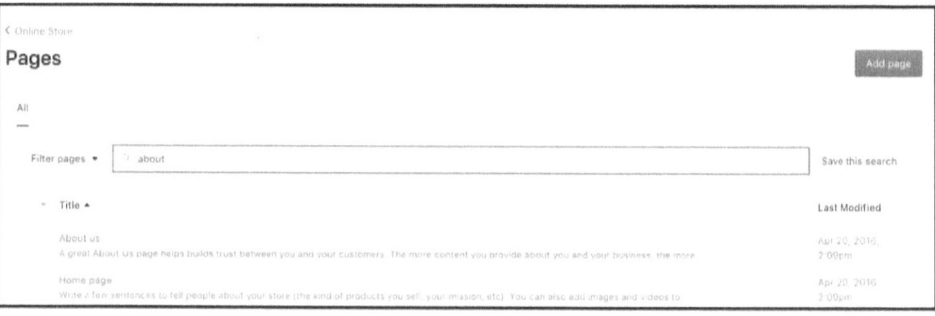

Again, this is very simple. Enter the title of the page, type in whatever you want to talk about on this page, and click **Save**. Voilà! Your webpage is created.

About your **About Us** page: Many websites ignore this page, but it is a crucial component of your online store. Lots of consumers visit the About Us page to learn more about the business and the story behind it. Remember, when it comes to marketing, story-telling is powerful. Consumers buy based on stories. Your story is also an opportunity for you to begin a relationship with your existing and potential customers.

I encourage you to spend some time to write a well-thought out About Us page. Share your story, your vision, your store's purpose, why customers should buy from you, why you are offering the products you are offering, and even share your personal story so your customers can relate to it.

Next, you also need to create a **Frequently Asked Questions (FAQ)** page to minimize the number of people emailing you with questions. When you create the FAQ page, you will type in all the general FAQ questions and answers that you can think of. Now, when people have a question, they can go there instead of calling or emailing you. Customers want answers fast, without waiting for a reply or having to pick up the phone to talk to some. This is why the FAQ page is important.

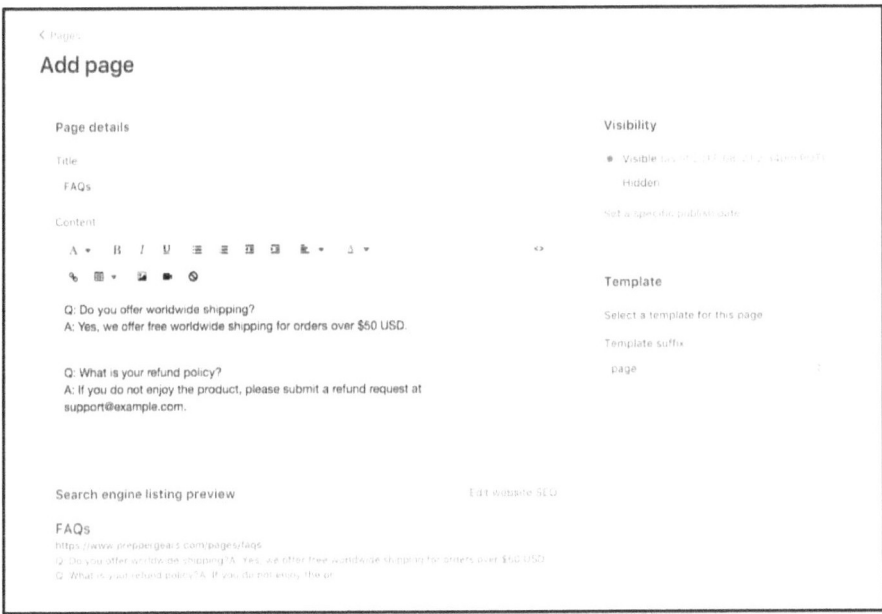

On both the About Us page and the FAQ page, you will include your terms of service, your privacy policy, your refund policy, and your shipping policy. To do this, go back to the **Legal section under your Settings,** copy your privacy policy, terms of service, refund policy and shipping policy, and paste them into an actual page. Why? Because right now, those policies exist only on the checkout form. You need these four pages on your actual e-commerce store website so that people can read them without having to check out.

Once you have copied and pasted these four legal pages, the final thing you need to do under Online Store is go to Navigation and add your privacy policy, terms of service, refund policy, and shipping policy pages to your Footer menu.

Then go into the main Menu and add your About Us page and your FAQ page.

Congratulations!

You have created your online store! Now it's time to add your products so customers have something to purchase. I'll share with you where to find products and how to take advantage of inventory arbitrage in a later section. For now, I'm going to quickly share how you can easily add products to your store.

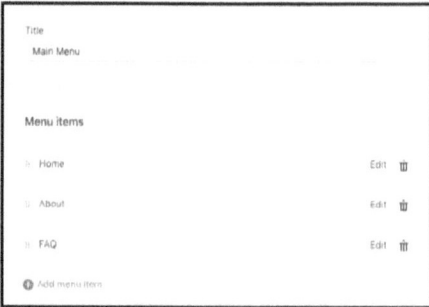

From the Shopify admin portal, click on Products in the main menu and then click Add Product. Again, this is very self-explanatory. Shopify has done a great job of making this fail-proof. Type the title of the product in the Title field and then type the information about that product in the Description field. This is where you tell your customers all about the product. What color is it? What does it look like? What does it do? What are the benefits for the customer?

One of the most important aspects of writing your product description is being sure to list the benefits. People need to know why they are buying it. They don't care about features. They care about benefits.

Let's use selling a pen as an example. You want to tell your prospects why they need this pen. They don't need the pen because it has black ink, and a 7-millimeter ballpoint tip. You don't want to say any of that. Instead, tell them the benefits.

Tell them, "This pen will allow you to write down all your important notes during your busy day. This pen will last longer than any other pen on the market because of the way the ball point is created." Those are benefits! Provide the benefits for the customer right in your product description.

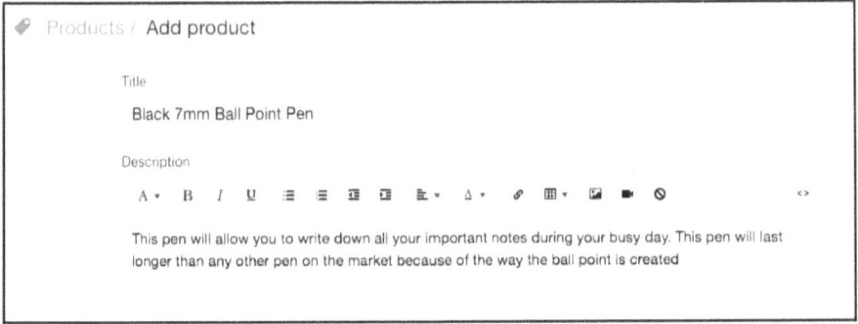

Next, under Images, just upload your product images. You can upload as many as you want. Put the image you want as your primary product image on the left; that is the one which will be the main image for your product. Then simply type in the price and the weight of the product, where the vendor is from, and the Collection in which this product can be found.

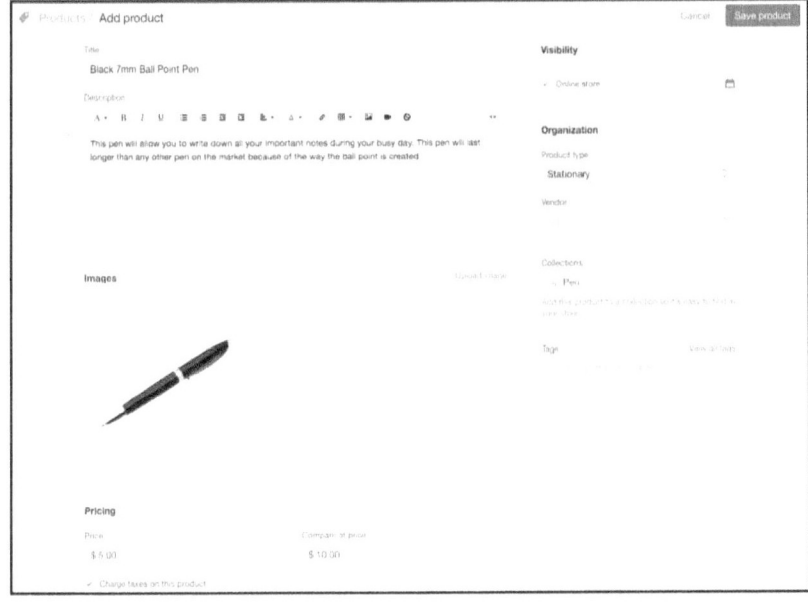

The Collection is essentially the product category. If it's going to be under accessories, is it under stationary? Is it under pens? Just put the product under the proper collection and click Save.

When you click Save, your product will automatically appear online - and people can actually purchase it right away. On the same page where you put in your information about your products, you can also add Variants if a product comes in different colors, materials, designs or has other options for customers to choose. Simply click the Add variant button and you'll be brought to a window which is self-explanatory once again.

Shopify Apps

Now that you have the basic understanding of how to add products, it is time to learn the importance of Shopify apps. I want to share with you four key apps that you absolutely must use. Again from the Shopify admin portal, Click on Apps, then click "Visit Shopify App Store". From there, you can browse the thousands of apps that Shopify offers to enhance your store.

Out of all the apps out there, there are only four that you need when starting your first e-commerce store. The first app is called Order Lookup. This Order Lookup is absolutely amazing! It reduces customer service requests by 80% because it gives your customers the ability to go through your website, enter their order number and their email address, and find the status of their order

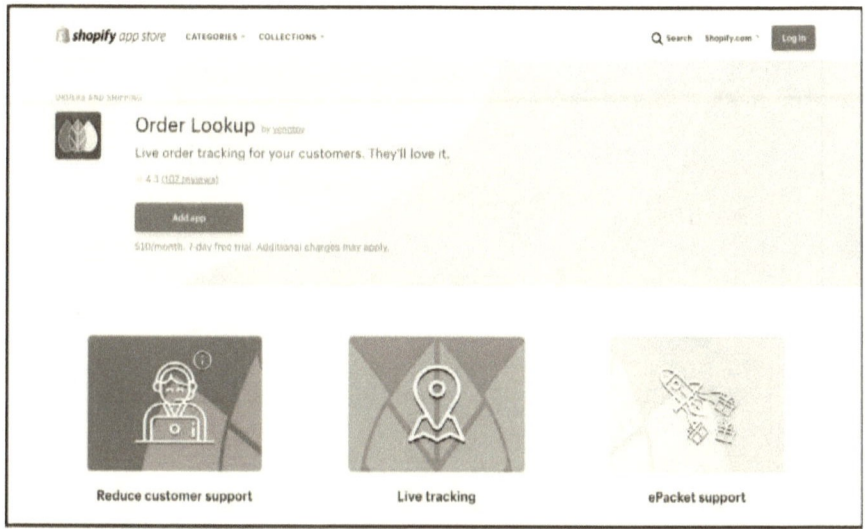

I'm serious when I say this.

When it comes to retailing online, many customers call or email to ask you where their product is and how long it will take to arrive. Fielding these calls and messages takes time. A lot of time. Order Lookup will minimize the number of phone calls and emails you get.

Order Lookup has a free 7-day trial, but afterwards it is $10 per month. I have to say, this $10 is totally worth it because you eliminate the headache and stress of dealing with repeated customer inquiries. As an entrepreneur, you want to focus your time on tasks that produce results. You did not sign up for a customer service job! So far, from your $100, you've spent $54.

The next app I suggest is called the GDPR Cookie Compiler. GDPR stands for General Data Protection Regulation. This is a regulation in European law on data protection and privacy of all individuals within the European Union (EU) and the European Economic Area (EEA). Since your store will be selling globally, it is wise to protect yourself from trouble. In this regulation, the use of cookies (small files stored on a user's computer which remember certain information and record the user's browsing activity) is carefully investigated. Having the GDPR Cookie Complier app will help you minimize your risk of non-compliance penalties and fees, and generally avoid getting in trouble with the EU.

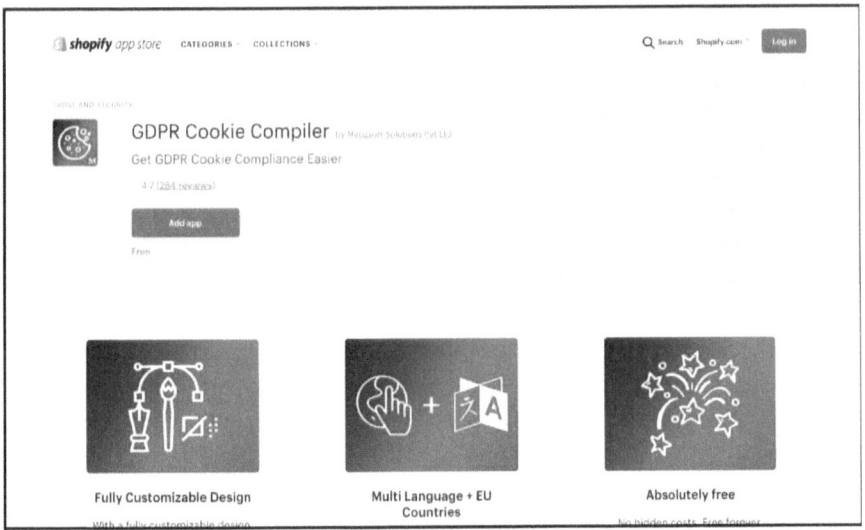

The next app I suggest is going to be a game changer for your store. It is called Sales Pop – Sales Notification by Cart Kit. The best part? It's absolutely free! I used to recommend Fomo, which does same thing, but Fomo starts at $19 per month. Comparatively, Sales Pop is a very decent free alternative.

As the name suggests, Sales Pop is essentially a real-time notification popup that displays each time a purchase is made on your store. It is an influential selling tool that gives social proof and credibility for your store, and helps to boost your sales!

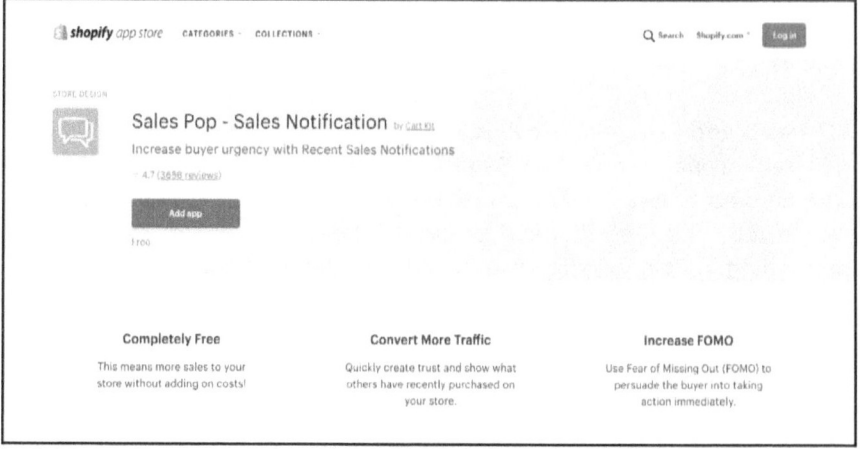

This is a very powerful sales strategy.

Seeing these popups will often trigger customers to think, "Wow, people are really purchasing from this website. I need to buy on this website because it is a legitimate e-commerce store and I can get my goods delivered to my door." This will dramatically increase your sales. It worked for me and it only costs you nothing so what is there to lose? I have made tens of thousands of dollars just by having this app installed on my e-commerce website.

The last app that I highly recommend you invest in is called Abandonment Protector Plus. It is only $8 a month, and believe me, it is worth every cent. The app allows you to send automated follow-up emails for prospects who abandoned their carts on your store. You have full flexibility on the design, content, and even timing of these automated emails, with the end goal of attracting these potential sales back to your store and convert!

One particular feature, Advanced Email Campaign, allows you to send automated emails based on the customer behavior, cart value, country, and even carts with particular products. This means you can send highly customized emails for your different audience. For example, you can tailor a free shipping message to your US customers and eliminate this offer to your international customers and vice versa. Or you can offer an irresistible promotion for prospects that are interested in a specific product to recover your sales!

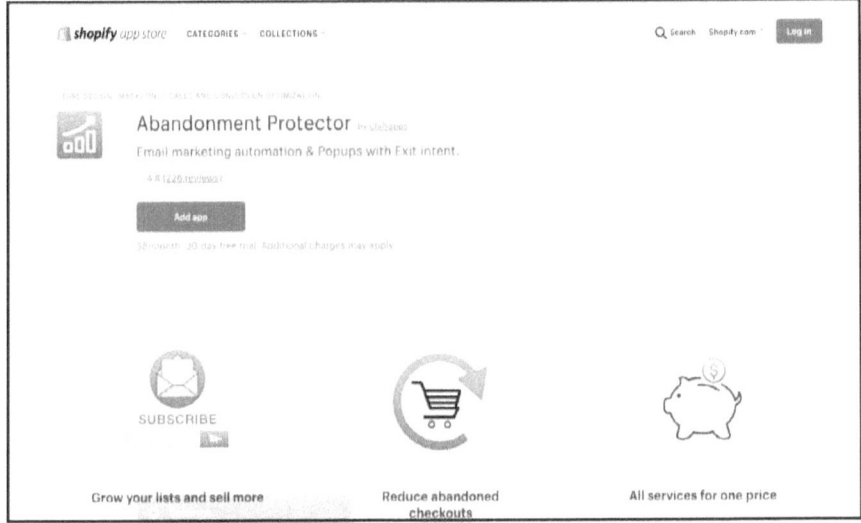

The investment you make in Abandonment Protector Plus is only $8, which brings the total cost of your e-commerce store so far to $62. I highly recommend you do this to maximize your average order value per customer. The more a customer comes back to buy, the more money you are going to make. This is exactly what Abandonment Protector Plus will help you do.

There are hundreds of apps in Shopify Apps, and you are welcome to go through them to see what other apps might be beneficial for your store. However, I don't recommend you add these right now because none is necessary in the beginning. Just stick with the four I have recommended to get your store up and running well.

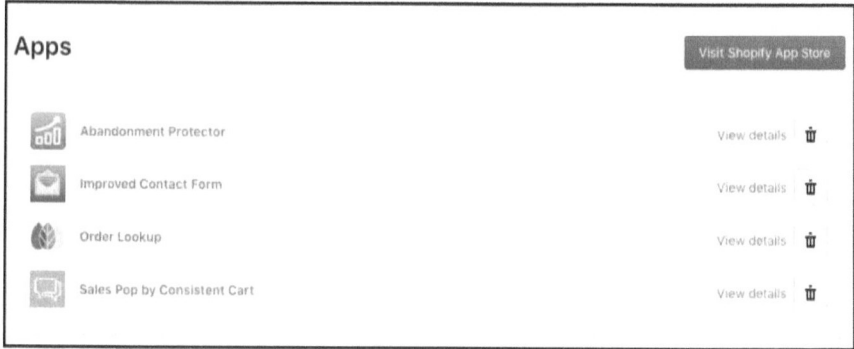

That's it! You now have a fully functional e-commerce store!

Now, there are two important items remaining. The first is processing customers' credit cards, and the second is inventory. I have a lot of fun, helpful information to share with you about inventory.

But first I'll dive in and talk about how to process customer credit cards.

Processing Credit Card Payments

Accepting credit cards online used to be a complete nightmare. You needed to have both a strong financial standing and a great relationship with your bank. On top of that, you would receive regular on-site visits from your banker, and there would be something to deal with called reserves. Reserves were essentially a hold on a portion of the funds whenever a credit card purchase was made.

When you processed a credit card online, the bank would hold 10% of the funds just to make sure they covered themselves in terms of risk. This way, the liability was not fully on the bank, but on you as well. Of course, the 10% reserve that the bank held would affect your bottom line because you would actually have to chase after the bank to release the remaining funds to you. Many banks would hold these funds for six months! As if that wasn't enough, you would have to have regular meetings with the banker - and the credit card processing fees were very high.

Fortunately, we are in an ever-evolving industry. For example, credit card processing changed drastically when Stripe payment was introduced to the market. Stripe was founded in 2011. It created a payment processing solution ideal for web developers, because it eliminated the need to register and maintain a merchant account with a bank. Stripe handles all the transactions, so it is a very easy way for you to accept credit cards. And the best part?

Shopify works closely with Stripe creating a payment processing method called Shopify Payments. If you have a Shopify store, you get instant approval on the processing of all major credit cards on your e-commerce store. You can process Visa, MasterCard, American Express, Discover, and Diners Club. There is no reserve - and you get daily deposits right into your bank account.

Stripe and Shopify have also teamed up on a very important chargeback feature. Let me share with you what chargeback means. If you see unauthorized charges or charges you don't recognize on your credit card statement, you can call the bank and say, "I did not approve this charge" or "I don't recognize this charge." When a customer does this, the credit card provider will reverse the charges and withdraw the money from your account until you have proved that the charge is legitimate.

Not so long ago, proving a charge was legitimate used to require a ton of workby the merchant (you). You would need to send all the related documents to your bank. You would need to contact your customers. You would need to fill out a chargeback form to make sure you have included everything that is relevant.

Those days are gone. With the Stripe-Shopify joint venture, you can enjoy using a very easy chargeback management tool. With just the click of a button, you can either contact your customer directly about the charge in question, or you can submit documents straight to your Shopify account to handle your chargebacks.

As with every other aspect of Shopify, it is very easy to set up credit card processing. Once you have logged into your account, click on Settings, and then click on Payments. Under Payments, by default, you will be prompted to use Shopify payments. All you have to do is activate it, enter your personal and banking information, and you will get instant approval on the processing of credit cards.

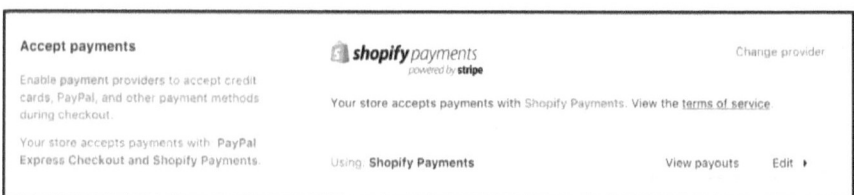

However, the downside to Shopify Payments is that it is restricted to certain countries.

You are automatically eligible to use Shopify Payments if you have residency in the following countries: Australia, Canada, Germany, Hong Kong, Ireland, Japan, New Zealand, Singapore, Spain, United Kingdom, and United States.

But don't worry. If your residency is outside of the countries above, simply speak to one of Shopify's live chat agents. They can recommend a provider based on your location. In my opinion, there are several options you can pursue. My first choice is Stripe. Stripe provides merchant processing to an extensive list of countries. You can check their website to see if your country is eligible. If Stripe does not have an option, then consider Payoneer or 2Checkout.com.

If none of those three options is available to you, then you can explore investing in Stripe Atlas to have Stripe incorporate a United States company for you to have access to merchant processing. It will cost roughly $500 but they take care of all the paperwork for you.

But processing credit cards alone is not enough.

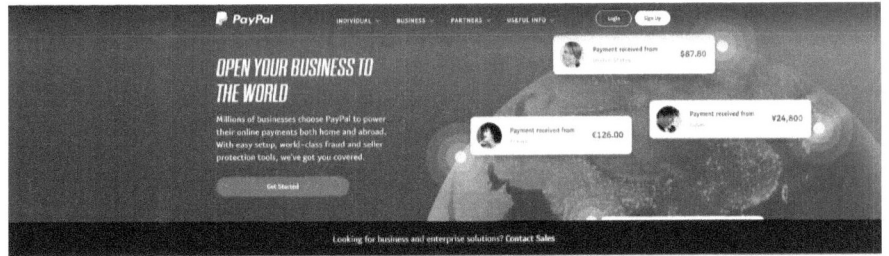

Reach more buyers and drive higher sales with PayPal

You will want to provide your customers with different payment options, including PayPal. You will absolutely need PayPal. Next, I will share with you the power of PayPal and why it is critical for you to get a PayPal business account to accept PayPal in your e-commerce store.

The Power of PayPal

As a new e-commerce store owner, you absolutely cannot ignore PayPal. It is one of the most powerful payment systems on the internet. Almost every e-commerce store accepts PayPal. This is why it is very important for you to accept PayPal in your online store.

Why is PayPal so important?

Let me tell you how it has benefitted me. Sales on my e-commerce websites have increased by nearly 20% just by having PayPal as a payment option. But don't just take my word for it. According to an Ipsos study conducted in July 2010 of 805 PayPal merchants, the merchants reported an increase in sales of 18% by doing nothing more than accepting PayPal on their website.

PayPal fees are very low. You don't even need to pay a monthly fee to accept PayPal payments. The fee for accepting payments starts at 2.9% plus 30 cents per transaction. From there it is a sliding scale; the more you process with them, the lower your fees are. PayPal fees can go as low as 1.9%.

But that's not all. There are over 267 million active PayPal users. That means people are very confident using PayPal to pay for their products online.

a lot of people actually feel more comfortable paying with PayPal than using their own credit cards. Why? Because PayPal has a protection plan in place for both buyers and sellers.

Accepting PayPal is another powerful way to increase the consumer confidence in your e-commerce store and that means your sales will increase.

Let me put this another way. The reason people feel more comfortable with PayPal is because they know that if they do not receive their goods, they can contact PayPal and get their money back. You just can't beat a deal like that!

In order for you to get a PayPal account, go to www.PayPal.com and sign up. It's absolutely free. You don't need to pay a penny to open an account. Remember to sign up for a business account because you get more advantages as a business than as an individual. This is especially the case if you are selling online. Once you have entered all your personal information, just enter your banking information and synchronize your PayPal account with your bank account. This allows you to withdraw your money from PayPal.

Another incredible advantage of accepting PayPal is that it now offers PayPal Credit (formerly called Bill Me Later). PayPal Credit is only for U.S. residents, but it is very powerful. If you have an e-commerce website that sells products valued over $99, your buyers will have the ability to use PayPal credit to purchase the product without paying a single penny in interest for six months.

Believe it or not, there is no charge for this!

PayPal Credit is a six-month, no-interest financing option that allows your customers to buy expensive products on your website without paying any interest. At the same time, PayPal handles everything for you! You don't have to worry about not being able to collect the money because all of that is PayPal's responsibility, not yours.

As a vendor, the benefit of PayPal Credit is absolutely amazing. If you are selling a very expensive product and the person either doesn't have a credit card or needs a financing option, PayPal handles it all for you.

Not convinced yet?

There is one last, mega, huge reason I recommend you accept PayPal. PayPal plays a huge role in scaling up your business, and I will share this with you when we get to Step 5.

For now, you have your logo, your domain, your website, and you can even accept credit cards and PayPal.

And guess what? Now it's time to look at inventory!

Chapter 5

The Inventory Arbitrage

Inventory? No Thank You

Finding inventory, finding new vendors, and finding your own products has always been one of the most exciting parts of opening a retail business. This hasn't changed, but with an e-commerce store, you can now cut out the middleman, thanks to Jack Ma and Alibaba. It is now possible for business owners to purchase directly from manufacturers. This is not how it used to be.

Not long ago, in order to carry a product, you would need to buy it through a third-party vendor who worked directly with the manufacturer. That middleman would mark up the margins and sell the product to you at a higher price than the manufacturer charged. They would make X amount of money by taking a cut for themselves, which would require you to set your prices higher.

Not anymore!

Now, thanks to Alibaba, you can buy goods directly from the manufacturer. This is where the magic of the margin comes into play. With this setup, you can really sustain your business and build it through profit. Just think: Instead of sharing 10% or 20% with a middleman, you are keeping that margin as pure profit for your business.

In their excitement, many business owners go to Alibaba, contact manufacturers directly, and find whatever they like. But the big shock comes when they place their order. They immediately get a hit with a minimum investment of $10,000, an investment that can soar all the way to half a million dollars! At this point, many dreams are shattered because it is so difficult to find the capital to invest in product.

At the same time, there are other entrepreneurs who are able to put down this kind of investment. Obviously, a lot of mom and pop shops need to buy inventory in order to survive. But they don't know what's coming. People think, "When I start a new business, all I really have to do is buy inventory." This is far too simplistic a way to view starting a business.

There are actually a lot of hidden fees and costs associated with purchasing inventory. Not only do you need to pay for the goods with a huge investment, you need to pay for the cost of freight shipment. Having the product shipped from the origin country to your country is expensive. Aside from the cost of transporting the goods, you will have to pay customs and duty charges. And on top of all this, you need to pay for packaging so the goods can be transported safely.

But adding up the cost of your inventory isn't over yet!

There is still another investment required. You have to find a designer to design your packaging and your flyers, and you need to buy these in bulk. The packaging alone costs tens or hundreds of thousands of dollars. Then you have to pay for warehousing and order fulfillment. You need to hire people or a third-party company to hold your inventory and fulfill your orders on a day-to-day basis.

Factor in all of these costs, and the cost of purchasing the product increases by a minimum of 20% over your initial investment. And you aren't even guaranteed a profit!

Now, let me ask you a few questions.

If you have invested a significant amount of money in your inventory, what if the product doesn't sell?

What if you purchase the wrong inventory?

What if the cost of investment is way too high, but you could have bought it for less through other sources?

There are just too many risks that many people are not willing to take. I know many people, including myself, who have invested a lot of money in a ton of inventory. We actually left it all in the warehouse. It's sitting there right now, collecting dust. We bought the product assuming it would sell, but ended up not selling a single item.

But this was the only option we had just a few years ago.

I knew there had to be another way.

And now there is a better way. If we all had to invest in inventory and bear this risk, then the number of entrepreneurs on the internet, as well as the number of physical retailers, would decrease drastically. But that's not what is happening! Instead, the number of online entrepreneurs is growing rapidly.

I know from my own personal experience that inventory is an enormous headache - and a major roadblock for many new entrepreneurs who want to create a profitable online business. Many of my own clients and associates told me that they were struggling to create an e-commerce store and keep inventory.

So I looked for a different method. I basically went on a journey. I tried to find the best possible way to have inventory, yet not have to invest a substantial amount of money in the beginning. I knew this would eliminate all the risk.

One day, I found the solution to this problem sitting right on my desk. It was an Amazon Package. As I looked at that package, I considered Amazon's business model. I took a deeper look. I mentioned earlier in this book that Amazon doesn't hold the majority of their inventory. Amazon is simply a platform through which people sell products.

Amazon collects the money, pays the vendor, and fills the orders.

Collects the   Pays the Vendor   Fills the Order
Money

I realized there must be a way to first collect the money, then pay for the goods and have the orders filled. With this method, you could make your money at the time of the sale. You wouldn't need to buy inventory upfront.

I knew that if Amazon could structure their business this way, I could too. I investigated further... and discovered inventory arbitrage. And now it is time for you to discover it too. Get ready to learn what inventory arbitrage is, and how you can take full advantage of it to build an online store with thousands of products. You can do it all without having to hold a single piece inventory - and you will minimize your risk.

The Inventory Arbitrage

You never need to hold inventory again !

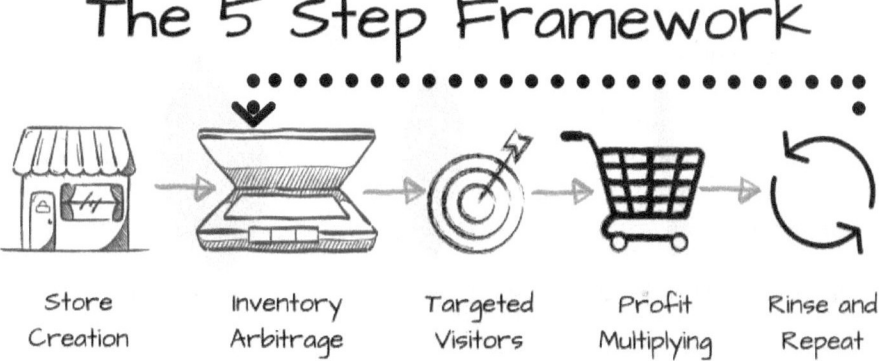

I know this is a bold statement, but I'm going to prove to you how you can use inventory arbitrage to sell thousands of products on your e-commerce store yet not have a single piece of inventory on hand. Not only that, but you can sell an exceptional variety of products across multiple categories.

Whatever you can think of, you can sell without the massive investment of $10,000, $50,000, or even half a million dollars just to stock your products. There are no more headaches associated with handling freight, making sure it gets on the boat, and gets safely to your warehouse. There is no more hassle of clearing customs, or paying customs duties or tariffs. You don't have to invest in warehouse space, and you don't have to hire anyone to fill your orders.

All of these inventory-related expenses and headaches are now history, thanks to my discovery of inventory arbitrage. Inventory arbitrage lets you sell millions of products, from watches to TVs to customized bracelets to clothing to literally anything that comes to your imagination.

And the best part?

You don't have to pay for any inventory until you have collected the money from your customers. Inventory arbitrage is also known as drop shipping. Here's how it works:

1. A customer purchases a product on your store and you collect the money.

2. The money you collect is a marked up price from your vendor. So, let's say you sell a dolphin necklace for $14.95, but you actually paid only $2 for this item from your vendor. This leaves you with profit margin of $12.95.

3. You take the $2 out of the $14.95 and set it aside.

4. You contact your vendor and have them ship the product under your name, so it looks to the consumer that the product is being shipped from your company, rather than from your vendor.

This entire process takes place behind the scenes without your customer ever knowing about it. All you are doing is arbitraging the inventory of your vendor by listing it on your e-commerce site and selling it.

Unlike traditional retail, you don't need to have the actual product on hand for the customer to grab and take to the checkout counter. All you need is the image and the product description. When a customer makes the purchase, youdon't even need to know if you have the product. All that matters is that the customer receives the item.

Now, Amazon isn't the only company using inventory arbitrage. A lot of online companies are basically arbitraging. They don't hold any inventory. Instead they act as the sales platform and have the vendor hold the inventory.

For example, I used to work in close association with a Car dealership. During the years I worked in that position, I learned a lot about how to create brand presence, and how to operate a retail store.

But how is working with a car dealership an example of inventory arbitrage?

A car dealership retails cars. You might think that a BMW dealership needs to hold a large inventory. But consider this: In India, BMW dealerships are held by private owners. They are not owned by BMW. A business person buys the BMW franchise and creates a dealership to sell the cars.

At first, I thought that all of these dealers had to pay hundreds of millions of dollars just to stock their inventory. But then I found out that they actually use inventory arbitrage. BMW headquarters gives a grace period to their BMW dealers on their inventory.

In other words, the dealers don't have to pay for their vehicle inventory when it hits their lot. Instead, they have a certain number of days to sell that inventory before they have to pay BMW for it. The cars are on the dealership's lot, but BMW still holds the inventory.

After a certain number of days, the dealer does have to pay BMW in full for the vehicles, to keep them on the lot and sell them. This is when many dealers go to the bank to get something called floor plan financing to pay for the inventory. This is a line of credit secured by the inventory itself. All the dealer does is pay an interest fee on each car, which really helps with the cash flow.

Obviously, the longer they have the cars on the lot, the more interest they pay. If they can sell that inventory very fast, they make profits right away. That's why many automotive franchises use floor plan financing. They are simply inventory arbitraging. These dealers are not holding their inventories; BMW or the bank is. This is a great illustration of the power of inventory arbitrage for your e-commerce store. Remember, your job is to build relationships with as many vendors as possible within your niche and then have the product available for sale on your store.

You can sell millions of products on your store. The sky truly is the limit, because all you are doing is investing your time to grab product images and enter product descriptions. That's it. You don't have to worry about the inventory because that is the vendor's responsibility.

Access To Millions Of Pieces Of Inventory

At this point, you may be wondering how on earth it is possible to have access to millions of inventory items without a spending a single penny to purchase them in advance. Not long ago, it was virtually impossible for this to happen.

Now, however, we are in a golden age of entrepreneurship. The internet has been evolving at such a rapid pace that this is the new reality of retail.

Now it is time for me introduce you to AliExpress. AliExpress was founded in 2010 as a subsidiary of Alibaba. It is an online retail operation made up mostly of small Chinese businesses offering products to international online buyers.

Essentially, the same manufacturers that work with Alibaba are selling items by the single piece at manufacturer's prices on AliExpress.

These vendors are used to selling products at wholesale prices. They understand that businesses who resell their products need to make a profit. That's why you can simply contact these vendors to set up drop shipping. Why are these manufacturers doing this? After all, wouldn't it be better for them to take bulk wholesale orders for their products? Yes, it would. However, a lot of Chinese manufacturers are suffering. It might appear to those in the Western world that these manufacturers make a lot of sales. But if you go to Guangzhou, you'll see a tremendous number of manufacturers closing each month. Their sales numbers are plummeting compared to five years ago.

That said, businesses that work with Alibaba needed to start diversifying, so they launched AliExpress and will do anything to acquire a sale. If you go to aliexpress.com, it may look like a retail store with an overwhelming number of items, but you can actually resell every single item listed on their site through your own e-commerce store with no inventory required. Just copy the product information and the product image onto your e-commerce store and start selling it.

It doesn't get any easier than that!

That's not even the best part. The best part is that with AliExpress you can literally sell anything! There are things you wouldn't even think of that you can sell: diaper bags, smartphones, security cameras, GPS systems, LED projectors, watches, and faucets. You can find just about anything through AliExpress. In fact, at one point I realized that AliExpress offers some products that are better than what we can get locally.

Take a look at this screenshot of a watch. You might think that this watch would cost $10 or $20 at a local shop, but guess what? Through AliExpress you can buy it for a mere 67 cents! It costs less than a dollar for this premium butterfly watch with rhinestones and a leather strap.

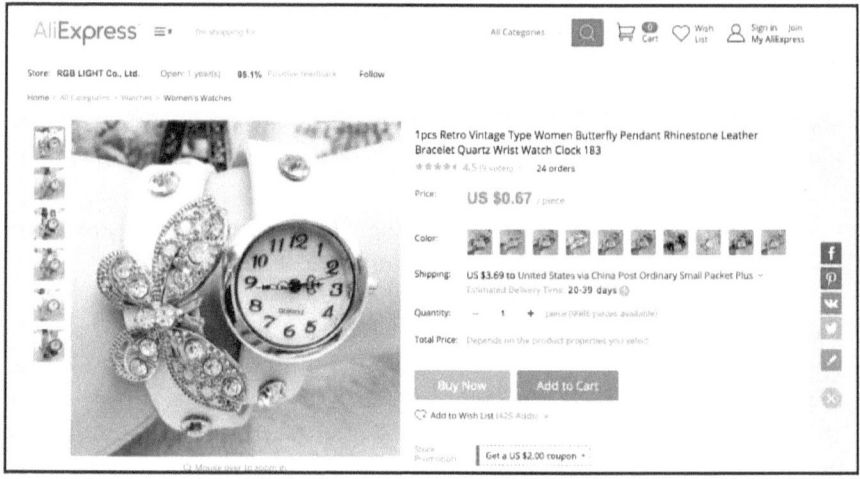

If you are a consumer and you see this watch priced at $9.95, you would think it was a pretty good deal. You might even buy a couple of them - maybe one for your daughter and one to give your niece for her birthday. The quality of this watch is actually pretty decent. It works perfectly fine and it is made with nice materials. And you can get it for only 67 cents.

If you sell this watch for $9.95, then you are making a profit of $9.28. Can you comprehend how massive a profit margin that is?

It is also extremely difficult to find this watch in a local shop. If a butterfly lover found the watch on your e-commerce site, obviously they would buy it.

This butterfly watch is just the beginning. There are tens of thousands of products that are priced lower than a dollar on AliExpress, and the perceived value is a lot higher than what you will pay for it. This means you can charge well over the wholesale price and sell these products via your e-commerce store, making a substantial profit.

Are you sitting there wondering, "What about the quality of these products?" (I know I would be wondering that if I were in your shoes right now!)

With AliExpress, you choose your products and your vendors. That means you can choose to work only with the vendors who provide quality products. AliExpress has even refined its system so consumers and buyers like you can see who the best vendors are, and whether a product is high quality.

Here's how. When you are searching for products on AliExpress, you first want to see the rating of the product and the number of orders it has received. Leveraging other buyer's review and rating will give you reassurance on the quality of the product.

Let's first look at the rating. The rating is out of 5 stars, just like ratings on Amazon. Ratings are given by real buyers when they receive the product to showcase its quality. I recommend that you choose products with at least 10 different buyer ratings showing an average of 4.5 stars and above. This will ensure both the consistency and the quality of the product. If the product has a lot of 1- or 2-star ratings, then the quality of the product may be low and you should avoid that product.

Next, make sure there have already been enough previous orders of the product. The product must have a minimum of 50 orders and at least 10 buyer ratings before I will consider selling the product in my store.

The last step to ensure you are working with the best product and vendor is to look for each store's positive feedback score and detailed seller rating. The positive feedback score is a percentage out of 100 which is driven by the three specific detailed seller ratings: Item as described, Communication, and Shipping Speed. Each of these detailed ratings is self-explanatory, with 5 being the best possible score.

Ideally, you want to work with a vendor that has a 95% or above positive feedback score and at least 4.5 out of 5 rating for each of the 3 details ratings. This will give you double confidence that the product is high quality and you are working with a reliable vendor.

When it comes to filling the orders for your customers, you might be tempted to use free shipping. This is not recommended. With free shipping, you won't have any tracking information for your product. If a customer contacts you asking where the product is, you will be forced to refund their money because you won't know. For this reason, it is very important that you pay for premium shipping.

When you choose premium shipping, ask specifically for ePacket. ePacket is a specific shipping method that China Post and USPS have created jointly to ensure faster shipping times between China and the U.S. You will pay between $2 and $3 per package. Keep in mind that you will be marking up the price of the product by at least 400%, and will have a high enough profit margin to afford this.

You can also charge the customer for shipping in order to cover the shipping costs. Many online customers are happy to pay for shipping; they understand that you need to put the product onto a plane, have the plane fly it across the ocean, and then have someone deliver it to their door. Whatever you choose, make sure your vendors accept ePacket so that you will have fast shipping. With ePacket, it normally takes two to three weeks for the product to arrive in the hands of your U.S. customer.

You can spend a lot of time on AliExpress just looking for the niche of products you have chosen to sell. Anything you can think of can be found on AliExpress.

Again, you can fill your e-commerce store with hundreds or thousands of products the day you launch, and you don't have to hold any inventory. All you do is copy the image, create a really amazing product description, and set the price. Then you can sell it on your e-commerce store.

This is why it's called inventory arbitrage; all you are doing is copying the image, copying the product description, and listing it on your store. You only buy the product from the vendor and have the vendor ship it directly to your customer when the customer gives you their money. That way you are collecting the money from your customer before paying for the product and you make a huge profit. You are using Other People's Money to build your business and that's the smartest way to run a business.

Just make sure that the vendor and the product have good feedback levels - and that they offer ePacket shipping!

Your goal is to get in the market as quickly as possible, and to reduce the time you spend finding products and uploading them to your store. But arbitraging AliExpress products can be a daunting and time-consuming process. Maintaining the products can also be a pain. The fact is that selling AliExpress products comes with several challenges. Let me familiarize you with each of the challenges of selling AliExpress products.

The first challenge is the time needed for uploading products into your store. Copying product images and uploading them into your store will take anywhere from 15 minutes to 30 minutes, depending on how many variants there are. If you want to add 5 products a day into your store, it'll take you several hours.

Second, each time you find a product that you want to sell in your store, you need to document the buy link on a spreadsheet. You need to be super organized with your vendor and product record keeping so that each time a customer orders from you, you're ready to quickly fulfill the correct product using the correct vendor.

The third challenge that you will encounter is the data entry work required whenever someone orders the product. Each time you receive an order and collect your customer's money, you will need to log into AliExpress, copy and paste your customer's shipping information, and pay for the order. If you are working with just a few orders a day, that is fine. But as you grow your business with more and more orders, this becomes a full-time job — a data entry job that you did not sign up for as an entrepreneur.

The last challenge is often overlooked but it can hurt your profit margins. Vendors often change pricing. At times, a product may be out of stock. Imagine you receive an order and payment, and then discover that the product is out of stock. Or imagine you receive an order, but then find out that the price went up drastically. This will cause you to lose money. Both of these situations can get super messy under normal circumstances. Just imagine if you happen to be promoting the product when it happens!

To avoid these situations, you need to stay on top of each vendor's product inventory and pricing on a regular, even daily, basis. If a product disappears from your vendor's stock or jumps in price, you may want to remove it from your store. This can get very time-consuming, or very sticky if overlooked.

Now, AliExpress is still the best go-to source for products for your store. You just need to stay on top of all these challenges. But if you want to eliminate all that time and work, and automate the entire process, I recommend you to checkout Shopzie at www.Shopzie.com.

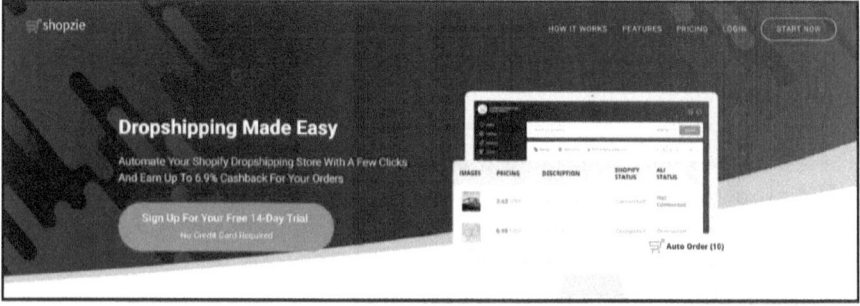

Shopzie is a brilliant tool that automates your entire e-commerce store. You can add products right into your store with a click of a button. All the images, descriptions, and variants are added to your store automatically, without you doing any copying or pasting.

Even the ordering process is automated and streamlined in Shopzie. Each time you receive an order, you simply log in to your Shopzie account and with a click of a button, all your customer's order info is added to your account.

Then simply enter your credit card information — and all the orders are automatically placed for you. When your vendor uploads the tracking information into your AliExpress account, Shopzie automatically sends this information to your Shopify account and notifies your customer so you don't have to. Shopzie can even alert you with real-time updates on what's going on with the products you are selling.

So, when the price on one of your products changes, or when a variant is out of stock, you get instant notification. This completely eliminates the need to review the status of each of your products on a continual basis.
I saved the best for last with Shopzie. Shopzie partners with AliExpress to give you up to 6.9% cash back for every order that's placed through Shopzie. That means you are making more while automating the entire process. As an e-commerce store owner, always remember that margin is king. The more margins you have, the more profit you make. It's that simple.

Shopzie is not free, however. Shopzie costs $19 a month, with a 14-day free trial that you can try. Now, I did not include Shopzie in your $100 budget because it's entirely possible for you to create your entire e-commerce business without Shopzie. It is up to you. But if I were starting a brand new e-commerce store right now, I would invest in Shopzie because time is of the essence.

To recap: When selling products from AliExpress, have all the checkpoints above checked for the vendors and products to make sure you are selling only high-quality products.

Sell Branded Products on your Store

What if your tastes are a little more refined and you want to sell brand name items?

Fortunately, AliExpress is not the only option when it comes to inventory arbitrage. When it comes to selling branded products, another option is doba.com. Founded in 2002, Doba is an American drop shipping aggregator which acts as a middle man between retailers like you and various drop ship suppliers. It all happens through a single interface. Again, you have access to over 2 million products and a massive number of vendors who are willing to drop ship products on your behalf.

Many vendors list their products on their members-only platform in order to drop ship their inventory. Doba requires you to have a subscription of $59.95 per month, but you can get a 14-day free trial to see what products are available before you commit to a membership. In comparison to AliExpress, Doba has great brand name products, such as NBA- or NFL-licensed products, Marvel products, Maxim, and as-seen-on-TV products. But remember, the cost of these products will be higher than what you get from AliExpress. This will eat into your profit margin and your store will be less profitable.

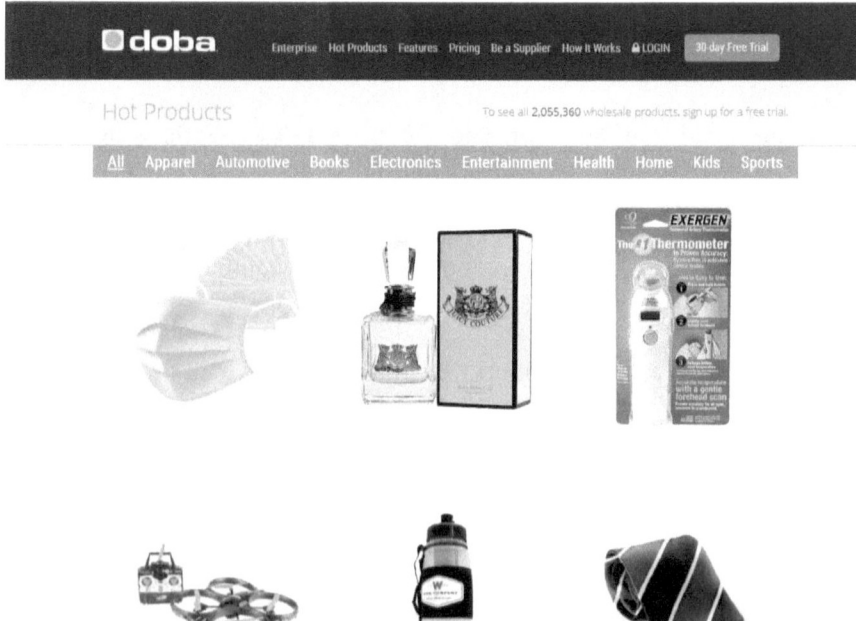

Does this mean you should avoid Doba? Not at all. And it doesn't mean that your store won't be profitable. It just means that you will have a significantly lower profit margin compared to AliExpress. With Doba, however, you can sell products in the thousand-dollar range; it offers many high-end, expensive products, such as 14-carat gold jewelry and outdoor patio sets.

But beware. I don't recommend that anyone just starting an e-commerce business to start with Doba. The products are priced high - and higher priced products are tougher to sell online. When the time comes that you want to expand your product line and showcase brand name items to look more legitimate and instill confidence in consumers, then I highly suggest you use Doba to scale up your business.

There are also more and more manufacturers and vendors around the world allowing you to dropship or arbitrage their inventory. You can conduct a Google search and find more. In all honesty, I believe that using AliExpress first is the easiest and fastest way to get started.

The Guide To Finding Winning Products to Sell Online

Now that you can see how you have access to millions of products to sell, it's time to make some important decisions. What products will you offer in your store? More important: How can you find products that will actually sell?

With so many products available, finding one that will take off like a rocket can be like finding a needle in a haystack. But don't worry. I've got some great tips to help you gain a competitive advantage and improve your odds of finding products that will sell.

Rule of thumb: Never sell products currently available in retail stores. Why? It normally takes months to stock a product in a physical retail store. By the time it gets there, it has already been sold successfully online — and your golden window of opportunity for online profits has closed.

Amazon

Your first step is to look at Amazon. We all know that Amazon is the king of e-commerce. You can literally buy anything on Amazon, and new products are being released continually. There's a secret passageway to find these hotselling items. Don't try to find it by navigating Amazon's website. Instead, go Google and search for **Amazon Best Seller**.

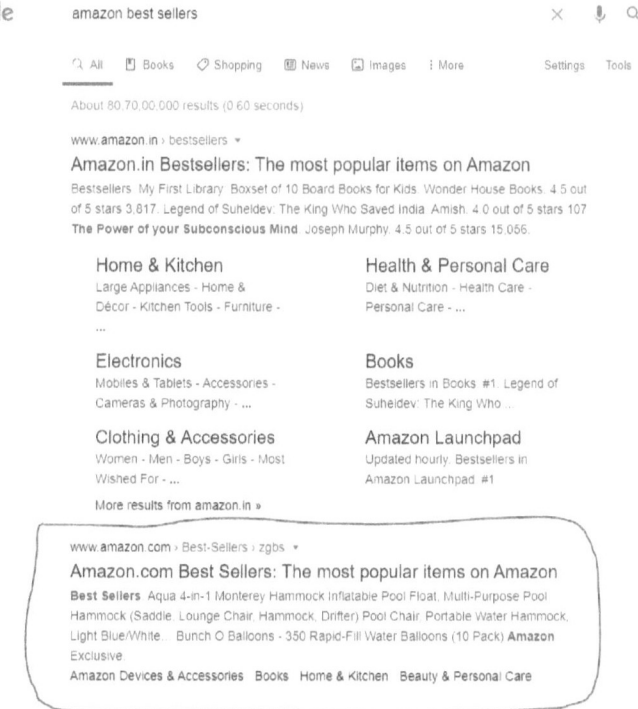

At the top of your search results, an Amazon page with a weird URL ending with /zgbs will appear. When you click that link, you will land on an extensive database list of Amazon's current best seller products, broken out by category

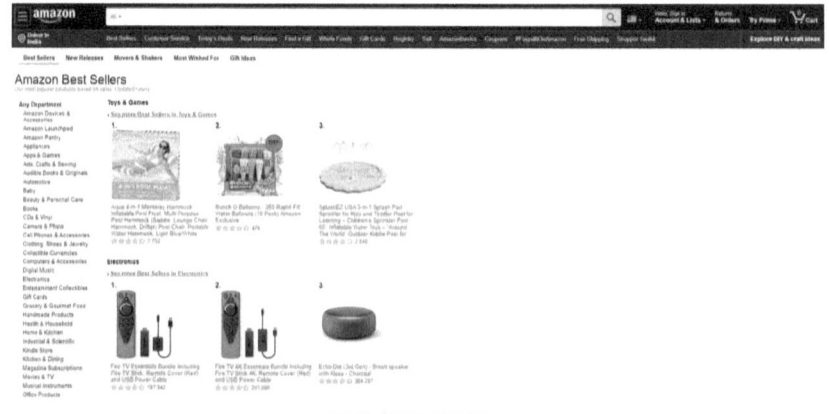

But don't stop there. This page offers a wealth of additional information to help you:

• New Releases
• Movers & Shakers
• Most Wished For

Let's look at the New Releases first. These are products that were recently added onto Amazon's database and that people are actually buying. This list is updated every hour so you can really see the latest products that are starting to take off. This lets you find trending products without any time-consuming research — and it's backed up by actual Amazon sales.

Next, the Movers & Shakers. These are products which have already been on Amazon for a period of time and have recently started to gain massive traction in Amazon's marketplace. This is a good place to look for products which weren't selling well in the past, but are suddenly selling due to a market shift.

You can capitalize on these products.

Last, the Most Wished For section is where you find the products buyers have added to their Wishlists or registries. These products are usually either more expensive than these buyers want to pay, or they're more desired than actually needed. With these products, you need to undercut the pricing. People love deals. When these products are shown to these consumers at a discount, they usually buy right away.

eBay

eBay offers you another way to find products that people are actively seeking. eBay started as an e-commerce marketplace where consumers could sell used items to other consumers. It has evolved into a full e-commerce platform where businesses sell unused products as well. To find the trends on eBay, use WatchCount.com. WatchCount.com is a third-party website that extracts information from eBay and shows the Most Watched items within each category. This lets you see what consumers want to buy on eBay and gives you a glimpse at products you can sell on your store.

Facebook

My last tip for finding great products — mining your competitors on Facebook — is by far the best. It may be a little complicated but it can let you find a winning product that may potentially lead you to thousands of sales.

As I mentioned before, social commerce is massive. While I write this, there are over 6 million active advertisers on the Facebook platform. This opens up a lot of opportunities for you to easily find products that are selling well in your niche. This is especially true now that the Cambridge Analytica incident has forced Facebook to be transparent about its advertisers. Take advantage of this and you can quickly and easily find a long list of products with high sales potential.

Here's how. First, log on to your Facebook account on desktop. Use the search bar with two goals in mind. The first goal is to find products being sold on Facebook and the second is to find competitors in your niche.

To find products sold on Facebook, simply enter the product you want to sell in Facebook's search bar, adding the following keywords: buy, discount, shipping, free, and save. These are the primary keywords that advertisers use in their Facebook posts. In the search results, click on the **Posts** tab and you will see several posts that are selling that product. Now look for high engagement and link to a store. The higher engagement, the more that product is selling.

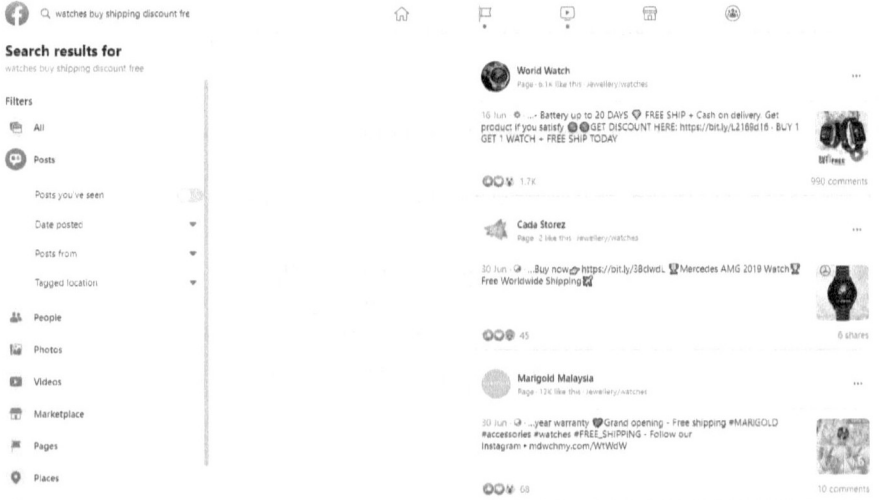

If, in your search results, you find a post which uses a bit.ly link, then you are in luck!

Bitly links have a little secret loophole which is super powerful for people like us. By simply adding a "+" after the bit.ly URL, you can see all the click activity including where the clicks originate. If the click volume is steady or rising, you've hit a jackpot. This is a product which is selling tremendously well.

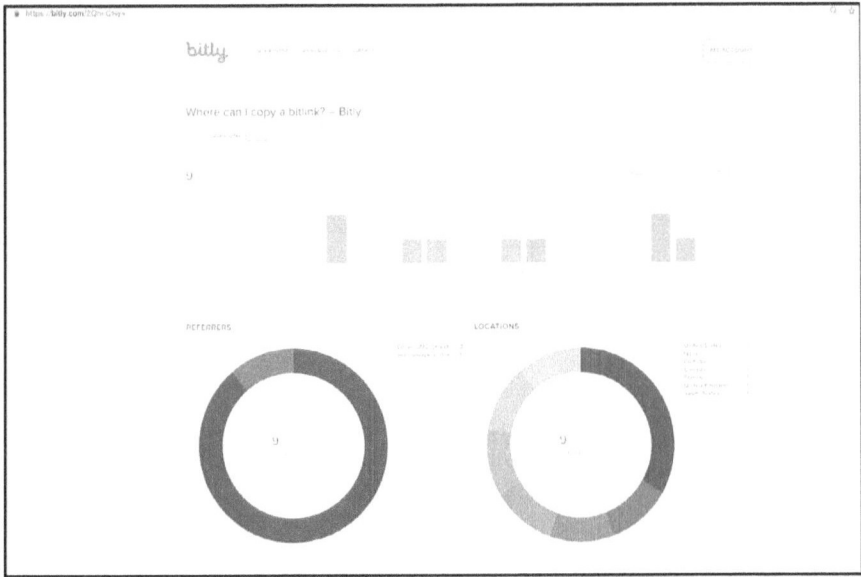

Don't use bit.ly for your own posts. Although it is proven to increase clicks and visitors to your store, you don't want your competitors to be spying on your sales. Plus, you can still accomplish the same results by using Tiny.ie. I fully endorse www.Tiny.ie and I highly recommend that you check it out and get a free trial account.

Now let's go back to your search results page. This time, click the Pages tab. To advertise on Facebook, you must have a Business Page. I will share with you exactly how to create one later in this book. For now, you'll use this to find other advertisers who are selling in your niche. The more competitors you find, the better. What I share with you next will completely change the landscape of your product research.

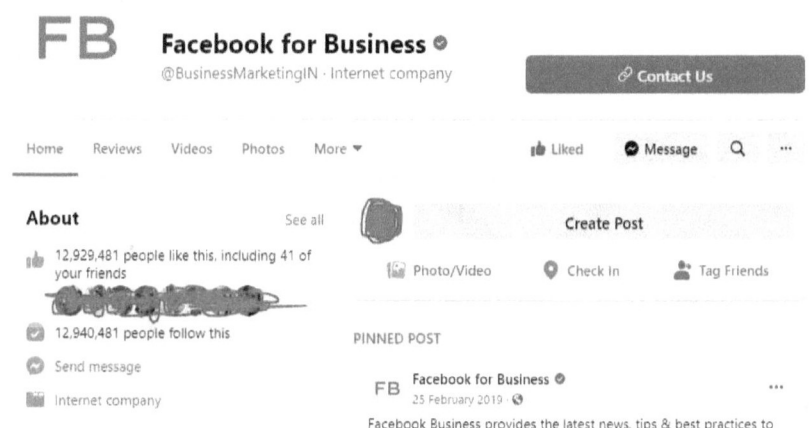

Click one of the competitor Facebook Pages. On the left-hand menu, you'll see a section called Info and Ads. This is gold. Due to Facebook's new advertiser transparency, we can now see exactly what our competitors are selling and stay on top of what is selling well. If you can find your competitors using a bit.ly link, then congratulations. You've won the lottery because you can now see what is (and what is not) selling for your competitors before investing time and ad dollars promoting a similar product. Remember: This is why you should not use bit.ly for yourself. Use Tiny.ie instead.

These tips put you on a quicker path to find the product to sell. Keep in mind: It is a fact that you only need one product that sells to potentially build a 6- or even 7-figure business. I have numerous students who achieved phenomenal results selling one single product. All it takes is doing your research.

The Pricing Formula

I bet you have been wondering for some time now how to set the prices for your products. How do you know how much to charge for a watch, a dress, or a smartphone? You have access to millions of products, but charging the wrong price will hurt your business. It is time to learn yet another skill set – the pricing formula.

Knowing how to price position your products is very important. This is knowledge you must gain in order to have a highly profitable e-commerce enterprise. If you price your products too high, customers will not be tempted to buy them, leaving a lot of money on the table and allowing your competitors take your business. At the same time, pricing your products too low will hurt your bottom line and the profit margin of your business.

Over the years that I have been operating e-commerce businesses, the magic number I have found when pricing my goods is 25%. The wholesale price you pay should be at most 25% of the price you will charge. For example, if you have a product that costs you $2.50, then sell it for at least $10.00.

Pricing your products, however, is not always a rigid rule, and this 25% pricing formula gives you a lot of flexibility. For example, you can create a sales event and discount certain products for a limited time. Just like a brick-and-mortar retailer, you can have a summer sale, a Christmas sale, a Father's Day or Mother's Day sale, or any other sale you want. You can take 40% or 50% off of the original price and still have enough margin to be profitable.

Another reason the number 25% will work is because you need to have enough of a margin to afford advertising. You see, no matter how much retail has changed, advertising is still the best way to attract consumers to your e-commerce store and turn them into customers.

Are you tied to 25%? Not at all. It is not a number that's engraved in stone. You will still need to do your own market research by visiting amazon.com, ebay. com, and etsy.com to see at what prices your competitors are selling.

For an even broader look at all the different stores on the internet that sell the same product, go to google.com, click on the shopping tab, and enter your product information. Provided the e-commerce retailers have synchronized with Google Shopping, you will see a showcase of all the businesses that are selling that product.

You have the final decision on pricing your product. The 25% formula is my recommendation based on my experience as an e-commerce entrepreneur. But if your intuition tells you that you need a lower margin to sell a larger quantity of goods, you can move all the way up to 50%.

I feel that 50% is the maximum you can afford. Anything over 50% will not leave you with much of a margin. Remember, you still have to attract consumers to your website, and that means you still have a few more operating costs. Pricing nearly every single product on your store at 25% will give you plenty of margin to be super profitable!

One last thing about your pricing formula: Perceived value.

Remember the butterfly watch? Based on the consumer's perceived value of the watch, it could sell for anywhere from $14.95 to $19.95. When consumers see it, they each have a price tag in mind - and that price tag varies. For this reason, when you are determining the price for a product, you absolutely must think of it as a consumer would.

What would you pay for it?

If you were shopping in a mall and you saw a similar product, how much would you pay? How much would the average consumer think it would sell for? Obviously, that perceived value is very important. Now, you can't sell that butterfly watch for $49.95. Sure, $49.95 gives you a huge margin, close to 90%, but people are not going to buy it because they won't see the value of the product as $49.95. The best approach is to price at 25%, go no higher than 50%, and really look at pricing in terms of perceived value.

Configuring Your Shipping

There is one final step to having a fully operational e-commerce store. Since you are selling a physical item, you need to factor in the price of shipping. Just like the pricing formulation for your products, shipping cost cannot be too high or too low. The sweet spot I have found ranges from $4.95 to $9.95 unless you are selling a very heavy item, like a big-box item. If this is the case, then you can stretch it to $14.95.

This pricing method for shipping is based on a single item. If a customer buys more than one product, they expect to pay more in shipping. However, nearly 70% of the time, a first-time customer will only buy one single item. That's why you should set your shipping prices based on single items.

There is one small kink. Thanks to Amazon Prime, we cannot charge too high a price for shipping. People are treated like kings when they have an Amazon Prime account. They get free shipping. Not only that. They have free two-day shipping! Sometimes, they even get free one-day free shipping.

Remember, you can price shipping too high. Again, based on my e-commerce experience in the past several years, $4.95 to $9.95 is the optimal range for most of your shipping costs. I promise. I have tried many tests to see the effect of shipping processes on my stores, and they always prove that $4.95 to $9.95 works best.

One final note on shipping prices…

On all e-commerce platforms, you have the option of using real-time shipping pricing. I don't recommend using this because you are not carrying your inventory. Because you are using inventory arbitraging, you need to have a fixed shipping price in your accounts and in your shopping carts. Here is the shipping table that I use for all my businesses. Feel free to copy and paste this right into your own store.

To create this shipping table in Shopify, click on Settings and then Shipping. You will now see a Shipping zone. In the Shipping zone, enter the shipping zone and the country that you would like, such as United States. Then edit the shipping rate by clicking Add Shipping Rate and following the table here. You can use this same shipping table for rest of the world as well because when you arbitrage inventory, your ePacket shipping costs are about the same around the world.

Weight based rates   Add rate

Name	Range	Rate amount		
Free Shipping	0 kg – 0 kg	Free	Edit	X
Lite Standard Shipping	0.1 kg – 0.19 kg	$2.95	Edit	X
Standard Shipping	0.2 kg – 0.29 kg	$4.95	Edit	X
Medium Shipping	0.3 kg – 0.39 kg	$7.95	Edit	X
Heavy Shipping	0.5 kg – 0.59 kg	$12.95	Edit	X

You don't want to get your shipping prices wrong and I don't want you to, either. This price range for shipping is what I can guarantee works fantastically well. Stick with it and avoid real-time shipping.

Now your store is fully completed! It's time to look at what you need to do next.

Chapter 6

"Build it and they will come" is False

What's in it for me?

The foundation is laid! You have pre-populated your e-commerce store with all the products you want (I recommend at least 25 products to start). Now is the time to consider the most important question of all: "What's in it for me?" This is the question that matters the most because it's the question every one of your prospects will be asking - whether they are aware of it or not.

When your prospective customers do their virtual saunter into your e-commerce store, they will be asking, "What's in it for me if I buy from you? Why should I buy from you?"

I'll be brutally honest with you. All people are selfish when it comes to buying online. It's true! They buy what they want - and only what they want. In a physical retail store, they may be with family or friends who pressure them one way or another. But in an e-commerce store, you simply cannot make use of the many emotional triggers that exist in a physical store. For example, physical retailers can play subconsciously manipulative music in their stores. They also normally employ sales people to convince you to buy their products.

When shopping online, people are not surrounded by these pressures and emotional triggers. For this reason, your sole job is to answer their one mental question, "What's in it for me?" Your prospects need to know the answer to this question because it helps them justify to themselves why they are spending their money to purchase something from you.

This is particularly true if they have never heard of your store before, or if your store is brand new.

Think about this. Would you buy something from your store? Why?

I know you have heard the expression "Build it and they will come." Please get that expression out of your head right now. "Build it and they will come" is a movie line, not a business model and certainly not a marketing strategy. If you think you can rely on it for your e-commerce store, then you have just built a sinking ship. Your store will fail.

Think about what you see when you do a Google search. It doesn't matter whether you are looking for information on how to plant a tree or for great birthday gifts for your father. When you conduct a Google search, you get hundreds of results pages - with millions of results!

Face it. The World Wide Web is a very big place! Your one little e-commerce website exists in a sea of billions of websites.

To really stand out and have visitors at your store, you need people to be able to find it. This means you need to craft an effective message (which we also call an offer) and broadcast it loud and clear so the public can hear you.

Your message is often the first impression consumers will have of your e-commerce store. For this reason, you must be sure that your message is very good.

But how do you craft a message to answer that all-important, number one question on every consumer's mind? There are two strategies you can use.

Messaging Strategy 1: Discounts

The first messaging strategy is to offer a discount. Everyone loves discounts. A discount message is even more effective if you make the discount a whopping 50% off the first item purchased. Why should you offer a 50% discount?

Because it is an **emotional trigger.**

And don't worry: Using the pricing formula discussed in the previous chapter, you will still make a profit even when you sell an item at 50% off. Now, when most people see a discount or a sale, they feel, "This sale is about to expire," or "This deal will be gone soon, so I have to buy this product right away."

Naturally, Shopify has an app that helps you create this discount offer. It is called Hurrify and it creates an emotional buying trigger. How? By creating a countdown timer on your product page! When people see 50% off and the time counting down to the expiration of the offer, their emotional buying trigger is activated. They think, "I better pull out my credit card right now and buy this product while I can still get 50% off!"

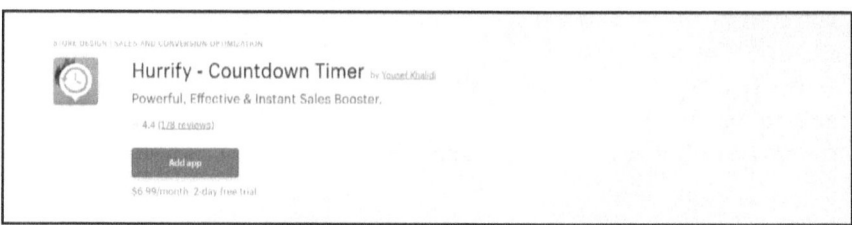

You see, factoring human psychology into the online retail experience is an absolute must for you to be truly successful. We already know that physical retail stores use many strategies that we cannot use online (such as playing music). That's why we have to use motivators like discounts and countdown timers to trigger people's emotions and sense of urgency.

Hurrify does this effectively, and there are other apps that work too. Hurrify isn't free, but it isn't expensive, either. It costs $6.99 a month. Even if you add another $6.99 a month into your budget, you are still well below the $100 cost of creating your e-commerce store.

Messaging Strategy 2: Free

The second messaging strategy is using the word "Free." People go absolutely nuts when they see free stuff! But don't panic; you won't simply give away product for free. That would cost your business a lot of money. So, how do you do it? Just charge for shipping and handling.

Remember, people already know that since they are buying a product on the internet, the product will need to be shipped. They will accept shipping and handling being charged to their credit card. When you use this method, choose specific products to offer for free. The best products to offer for free are the ones that cost you between $3 and $5.

When discussing free products, I want to be clear that we are not talking about "Free trials." Free trials are often offered on cosmetic products or nutritional supplements. This free trial strategy initially charges the customer only for shipping and handling, and then 14 or 30 days later, the seller charges the customer's credit card for the price of the product.

We are not using this free trial strategy. Our "free" strategy involves simply giving the product away for free and charging for shipping and handling. The price range of the free product is very important.

If your free products cost you between $3 and $5, and you charge $9.95 for standard shipping, then you still make a profit for that product. Many people, including my own students, are using this free-plus-shipping method. They are building seven-figure empires simply by giving away free products.

Messaging Strategy 3: Discounts + Free Shipping

Consumers love free shipping because it makes them feel like they are taking advantage of businesses. Offering free shipping also eliminates shipping cost an excuse for them not to buy from you. So when you combine a discount with free shipping, your offer becomes irresistible and consumers whip out their credit cards.

Use these three strategies to broadcast your message to consumers and to provide them with the best answer to their "What's in it for me?" question. These strategies let you shout out to the public, "Hey, come to my store right now and you will save money!" Saving money always draws consumers in. With you, they will get either a discount or they will get the product for free - plus shipping and handling.

Why is a Times Square Lease so freaking high?

You now have a marketable offer, so it's time to master the third step of my 5-Step System: traffic!

I'm not talking about the traffic on the street outside your house or work. I'm talking about the virtual traffic of website visitors to your online store.

When you create an e-commerce website, you, along with billions of other website owners, own a tiny piece of real estate on the internet. To generate revenue, you need traffic by website visitors. The more traffic you have, the more sales you make, and the bigger your brand becomes.

But what do I really mean by traffic? I'll use the example I have used many times to educate people around the world on the concept of traffic.

For now, think of your e-commerce store as a physical store. Where is it located, exactly? There will be a huge difference in the amount of money you pay for a leased space in New York City's Times Square versus a space in the hot desert outskirts of Las Vegas. When you open a retail store in Times Square, it will cost you hundreds of thousands of dollars, whereas if you open it in the middle of the desert, it will cost you less than a thousand bucks a month.

Why is there such a drastic difference in these lease prices? Traffic.

The more foot traffic of people walking past your storefront, the more you will pay for a lease. It makes sense. How many times have you walked into a store simply because you happened to be walking past it and thought it looked interesting? You're not the only one who has done this. The more people walking past a store, the more valuable the location.

This is why places like Times Square, or even a mall in your local area, cost a fortune every single month. Auditors actually go to these locations to determine how much foot traffic there is in front of a retail outlet. They mathematically calculate the lease rate based on the amount of traffic. So when it comes to a physical store, you need to make a significant investment every month on your lease. This cost is directly related to the amount of foot traffic around your store.

How does this work on the internet?

Obviously, it's not quite the same. There isn't a stream of potential customers walking by all the time. You simply don't have that privilege. What you do have is the ability to advertise your website and offers to drive traffic to your store.

To start generating sales, you need to master the art of generating traffic. You take the funds you would use to pay for a physical store lease and instead use them to advertise your website.

"Generating traffic is an art.
In the online world, Traffic
is King"

It is not something that you can master overnight. However, in the next few sections I'm going to share with you how to do it - so you can literally generate traffic to your site in the blink of an eye.

Importance of Traffic

I'll say it again. In the online world, Traffic is King !

The more you know about how to generate traffic, the more sales you will have. It really is that simple. I like to define traffic using classic Greek columns. If you take a look at the depiction below, you will see that the top of the building is like a rooftop. This rooftop is your business and the traffic that supports that rooftop is represented by the pillars below it.

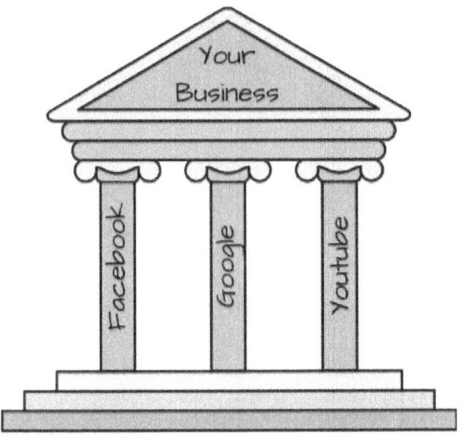

Each stream of traffic is represented by a pillar. The more pillars you have, the larger your income stream, because each pillar of traffic translates into sales. Additionally, the more pillars you have built, the more sustainable your business is.

If you only have one source, or pillar, of traffic and something happens to it, your business simply cannot stand. You simply cannot rely on only one source of traffic. You cannot put all your eggs into one basket. If you do, your business will collapse. It will not be sustainable.

This illustrates why your job as an online entrepreneur is to create as many pillars as possible to sustain the business. With several sources of traffic, you can continue to sustain your business even if one of those sources flops or dries up.

Now that your entire e-commerce website has been created and loaded with inventory, you need to start building your pillars. In the next section, I'm going to share with you the three ways of generating traffic that will turn you into a traffic guru.

But first, you need to know that when you master the art of generating traffic, you can actually charge other companies or small businesses a fortune to help them generate their own traffic.

The ability to generate traffic is the number one skill set that I developed during my career. This is the expertise for which I'm known. I also created a company, Designate, that specializes in increasing Returns on Investments for entrepreneurs like yourself by implementing extremely sophisticated techniques to derive the full potential revenues and profits for your business

Since you cannot sustain your business without traffic, and you need traffic to generate sales, I am now going to teach you how to turn traffic into profit. I'm not talking about a little bit of profit; I'm talking about a serious amount of profit. I'm going to share with you how you can gain access to the multi-billion traffic source network starting with just $5.

Let's Get Started

The 3 Ways of Getting Prime Traffic

There are many ways to drive traffic to your website. One popular technique is SEO, or Search Engine Optimization. SEO is popular, but it's not terribly feasible. It's a very difficult way to generate traffic. Despite this, many people are teaching how to use SEO for traffic generation. In brief, SEO is based on the use of keyword density on your page. You build your site with content that is keyword-optimized. Then you list your site on Google, Yahoo, and Bing and hope that it will appear on the first search result page when users type your keywords into the search bar.

Another option is forum posting. This entails going into related forums, posting comments and valuable content about your business and your products, and hoping that people will click on your link to take advantage of your offers.

Yet another method of generating traffic is article marketing. With this method, you write articles on a day-to-day basis and submit them to article websites.

All of these options can be very tedious. In this book, I am not going to share with you how to do these things. Why not? Because the reality is that these methods are very difficult, requiring a lot of time and effort to gain some traffic.

I have a better way. Three better ways, actually.

In this chapter, I am going to reveal these top three methods so that you can use them to start generating instant traffic in your online store.

Method #1: Social Media

It is incredibly important for you to leverage social media to drive traffic to your website. Not sure what social media is? You probably use it regularly without realizing it. Social media are basically platforms in which people engage and interact on a personal level. Smart businesses are taking advantage of social media to build their brands and generate traffic. They use their presence on social media to share information and offers about their products, their content, and related items that consumers need to know.

Using social media to promote your business is now called social commerce. Social commerce offers a very big market in our industry, one that will continue to grow in the years to come. It allows you to leverage social media to get visitors to your e-commerce website to acquire sales.

Now get ready for a mind-blower. I am going to share a statistic that literally blew me away when I first saw it. This statistic gives you a glimpse at the impact of social media for driving traffic to your website. This statistic comes from Shopify, the provider we are using for our e-commerce website.

Shopify conducted an analysis to determine which social platforms drive the most sales. It looked at 37 million website visitors who came from social media and converted into 529,000 e-commerce orders. Shopify looked deeply into its database to get this data. It looked at Facebook, Twitter, Pinterest, Google+, LinkedIn, Instagram, Reddit, YouTube, Vimeo, Vine, Hacker News, and Polyvore.

The statistic? 63% of the 37 million visitors were driven by Facebook. That translates into 23.3 million people all driven by Facebook.

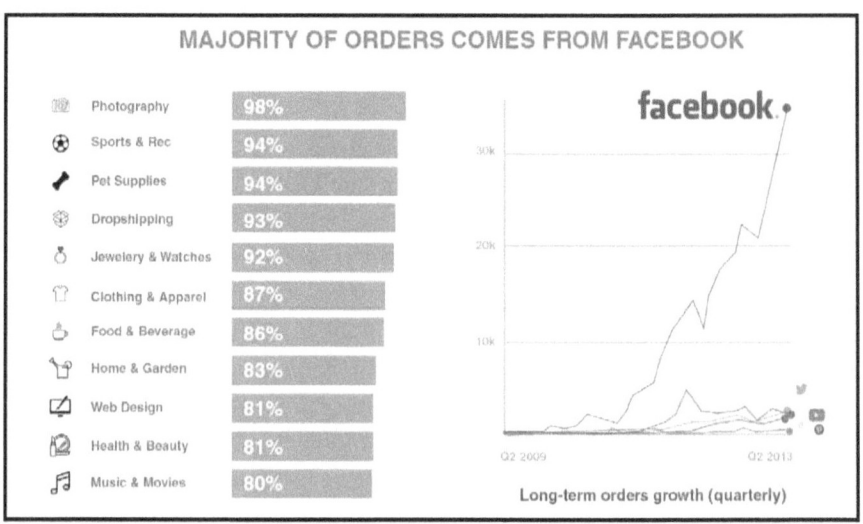

Facebook essentially owns the entire market share!

What does this mean for you? If you use Facebook, Pinterest, and Twitter, which, when combined, account for more than 87% of the market share, you will start getting sales at a much faster pace.

The craziest part is that, on average, 85% of all orders from social media belong to Facebook. In fact, Facebook dominates some industries such as:

• Photography
• Sports and recreation
• Pet supplies
• Jewelry
• Clothing
• Food and beverage
• Home and garden

If you are in these industries, you need a Facebook presence.

Another surprising result from this analysis showed how much people spend on Facebook. I can virtually guarantee that you or one of your friends or family members has bought something via Facebook - and the average order value on Facebook is $55.

That means that if you take all the social media orders, 85% of which are via Facebook (that is, 85% of 529 thousand e-commerce orders that stem from social media), you're looking at nearly $25 million in sales right from Facebook.

You definitely need to have a presence on Facebook!

Another fast-growing social media platform is Instagram. I suggest you get an Instagram account, a Pinterest account, a Facebook account, and a Twitter account for your business. These four alone will give you a huge head start over many other new e-commerce brands.

We are going to start with a focus on Facebook, partly because of its dominance in social commerce and partly because the other platforms are so similar to it.Once you understand how to market on Facebook, you will easily be able to do the same on Twitter, Instagram, and Pinterest. In fact, if you build a foundation on Facebook, you can take whatever you post on Facebook and apply it to Twitter, Instagram, and Pinterest.

So, you know Facebook, right? You are on it every day. How hard can it be to use it as a way to market your e-commerce store?

The main difference is that you will be creating a Facebook page for your Business. Fortunately, this is very simple to do, and it's free. All you have to do is log into your personal Facebook account and under the Create section on the left-hand navigation menu, click on Page.

Create

Ad · Page · Group · Event · Fundraiser

Once you click this, you will be asked to choose a category for your Facebook page. Facebook has simplified it so you can either select Business or Brand OR Community or Public Figure.

Since you are trying to develop an eCommerce store, you should select Business or Brand as the category and click on the Get Started button.

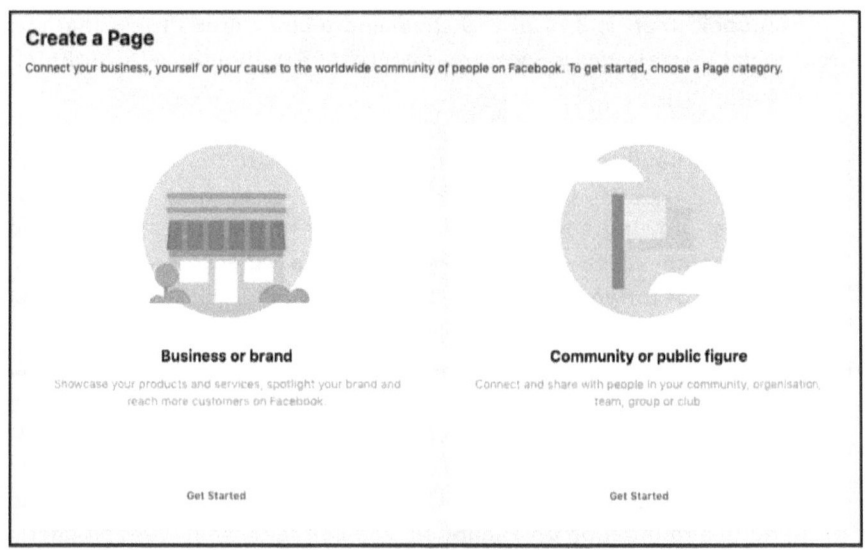

Create a Page

Connect your business, yourself or your cause to the worldwide community of people on Facebook. To get started, choose a Page category.

Business or brand

Showcase your products and services, spotlight your brand and reach more customers on Facebook

Get Started

Community or public figure

Connect and share with people in your community, organisation, team, group or club

Get Started

Next, enter a Page Name and select a Category to describe your page. The Page Name should typically be your business name or brand name. As for the Category, type in one or two keywords to describe your store and it will populate a drop-down menu for you to select a category. You can either enter in your niche or simply say that this is for an e-commerce website. Once you're done, click on **Continue.**

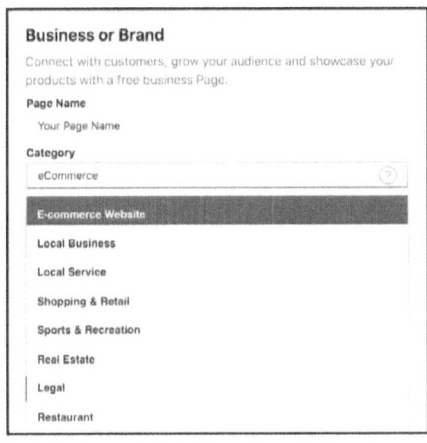

Next, upload a profile picture for your Facebook page. You can skip this step for now and add it in later if you don't have an image ready. Please keep in mind that the recommended upload size for your Facebook profile picture is 180 pixels wide by 180 pixels tall.

Then, upload a cover photo for your Facebook page. Again, you can skip this step for now and add it in later if your image is not ready. The recommended upload size for your cover photo is 828 pixels wide by 315 pixels tall.

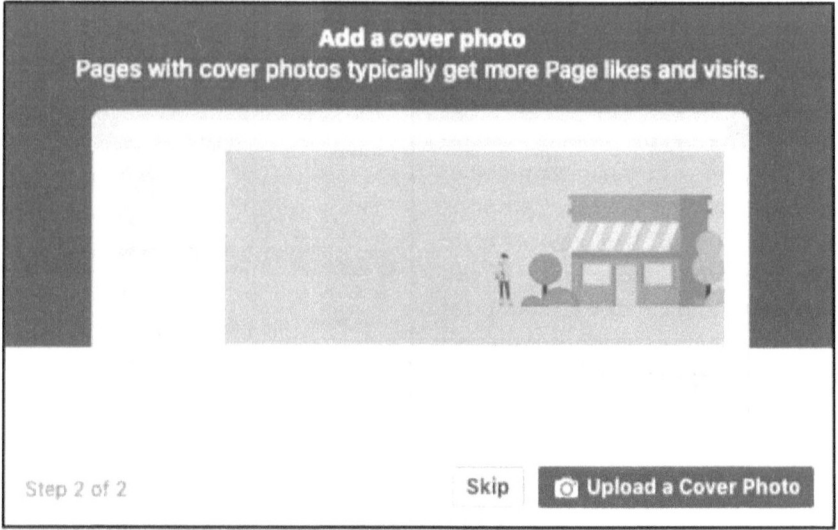

That's it! You have officially created your Facebook page!

Obviously, there are a lot more information you can add to spice up your Facebook Page. You can do that in the About section.

I also recommend adding a Shop Now button under your cover photo, which will bring people to your store. Then start inviting your friends to Like your page. This will help it go viral, which is exactly what you want to do on all social media platforms.

Going viral is key!

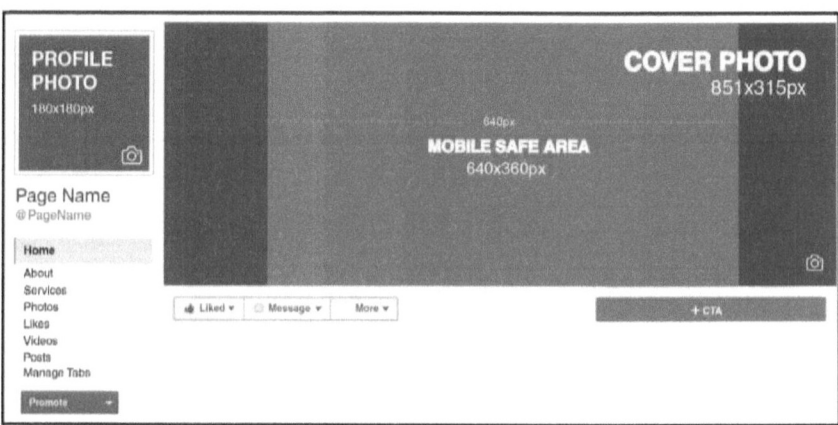

How do you go viral? It's all about the content.

It means you will post unique viral content on a daily basis, content that will sometimes include promotional content. Every day you will create posts related to your niche. These can be posts on:

• Important news
• Important people
• Customers using your product (If you can get customers to send in photos,
this is great!)
• New or feature products
• Current promotions
• Anything else related to your niche and your e-commerce store

In order for you to gain some traction on Facebook, you need to start liking other people's pages, particularly pages that are related to your niche. Comment on people's posts. Say, "Hey, I have a special offer, go check it out." You want to leverage the social media platform through engagement and create conversations with people so they can tag your page, like your page, and share the contents of your page. That's how you will start generating traffic through social media.

It is vital that you have a Facebook page in place. Once you have this up and running, I would suggest you set up your Instagram, Twitter, and Pinterest accounts. Then link these pages so that your followers can follow you on all of your social media accounts. This will help you create an even bigger following!

Instagram

Instagram has been growing at such a rapid pace that all e-commerce marketers need to know about it. It has now surpassed a total of 1 billion active users and continues to grow every day. The best part about Instagram is its organic reach and user engagement of hashtags. You can and should take advantage of this.

Once you have created a Facebook Page for your store, the next step is to create an Instagram Business Page. Start by getting the Instagram app on your smartphone. Then follow the tutorial to create an account. Once your account is created, head over to the bottom right-corner tab, click your icon, then click the top-right corner menu icon. From there, you will see the Settings tab. Scroll to the Business Settings and switch your account from a Personal Account to a Business Account. It's that simple.

Now, let me share with you some tips on what and how often to post on Instagram. It's important to understand that the Instagram ecosystem works by connecting people and highlighting their bright side. Leverage that by using lifestyle photos in your posts. Lifestyle photos are pictures of your product in a real life scene. This might be showing someone using the product, the product sitting in the grass, or another image which connects with our everyday lives. If you are in the fashion niche, for example, you don't want to post a plain picture of a dress. Instead, post an image of someone wearing the dress.

As you are posting your pictures or videos on Instagram, make sure you include well-thought out text about the product. Use stories to sell. On Instagram, people are more likely to buy something that's sold through a story-telling format than through a direct response buy-buy-buy message. Wrap a story around the product you sell and encourage feedback and comments. The more engagement you have on your post in the first hour, the more likely it will be featured on the explore page for your potential customers to see.

Use hashtags in your posts, but don't include them in your post text. Simply create your post, and then reply to your own post with hashtags that are relevant. Aim for 7 to 10 hashtags maximum and keep them as tightly-themed as possible.

Finally, post at least 3 times a day on Instagram: in the morning, afternoon, and night. This will allow you to reach as many people as possible with your message. Start attracting followers and making sales by posting regularly and showcasing the products that you are selling in your store. As your following grows, Instagram will become a true asset to your business.

Method #2: Influencer Marketing

Influencer marketing is now a powerful way to sell products. Basically, influencer marketing is having an influencer or an online celebrity showcase and endorse your product. Have you heard of Kylie Jenner? She is now the youngest self-made billionaire because of her influence on her followers. In the first hour after she released her Lip Kit cosmetic product for $29, it raked in millions of dollars. In just a few years, she has built a $900 million fortune from it. This is all due to her influence on social media.

But you don't need to be a celebrity or have a ton of followers to snatch a piece of this pie. Instead, you can leverage other people's influence to your advantage.

There are tens of thousands of influencers on Instagram and YouTube that you can pay to get a shoutout or endorsement for your product. These shoutouts or endorsements cost anywhere from $10 all the way to hundreds of thousands of dollars. Don't start with shoutouts that cost thousands or even hundreds of dollars. Start small to test the water first before you proceed into finding bigger influencers.

When working with influencers, the best way to start is through Instagram. Simply conduct a keyword search on influencers specific to your niche. On a spreadsheet or a piece of paper, list these influencers or Instagram names as long as they have a minimum 100,000 followers. Then go into the Instagram page. Right under the metrics, click the drop-down menu to find similar influencers or Instagram pages related to the ones you've listed.

Now it's time to find out whether these influencers accept promotions. Look at each bio description to see if there's any way to contact them. Most will ask you to DM (direct message), KIK, WhatsApp, or email them. If they provide a contact method, they will usually accept shoutouts. That's how they make their money.

But before you contact anyone, ensure they have real fans, not bots. To do so, all you have to do is take a look at their most recent post (hopefully yesterday). Add together the number engagements and comments for that post. Divide that number by their total number of followers, then multiply that number by 100. If the resulting engagement rate is over 1%, then you know their followers are legitimate. These are the influencers to contact for pricing.

Now go ahead and contact the influencer using the contact method shown in their bio. Once you've sealed a deal with them, send them your product so they can do a shoutout for your store and product. Always use a Tiny.ie link to track the performance of your shoutouts so you know which influencer actually produces results for you and which doesn't. Continue to work with the influencer who produces results.

You might be thinking, "OK, social media and influencer marketing look great, but they are either going to be time consuming, or they're going to cost me a lot of money."

Well, there is one more method that you can use. Using this third method alone, I can virtually guarantee that you can start making thousands, tens of thousands, or even hundreds of thousands of dollars.

Method #3: Facebook Advertising

This method is so easy that there isn't much to say about it, except that it is the best! I will go over this method in more detail in the next chapter, but here I want to tell you that Facebook's self-service advertising platform has ushered in a new age of advertising. You can start advertising your products for a mere $5. That's it! With just $5, you can start advertising your product and potentially make a profit right away. That's another $5 of your $100, which brings you up to $73.99.

You might be thinking, "I'm probably going to end up spending a lot of money on advertising." No way! Listen and let me reassure you: You really don't need thousands or even hundreds of dollars to start advertising on Facebook. All you need is $5.

What's more, I am going to help you minimize your risk by sharing with you, step-by-step, how to set up your Facebook advertising campaign so it will generate traffic and sales for your e-commerce store.

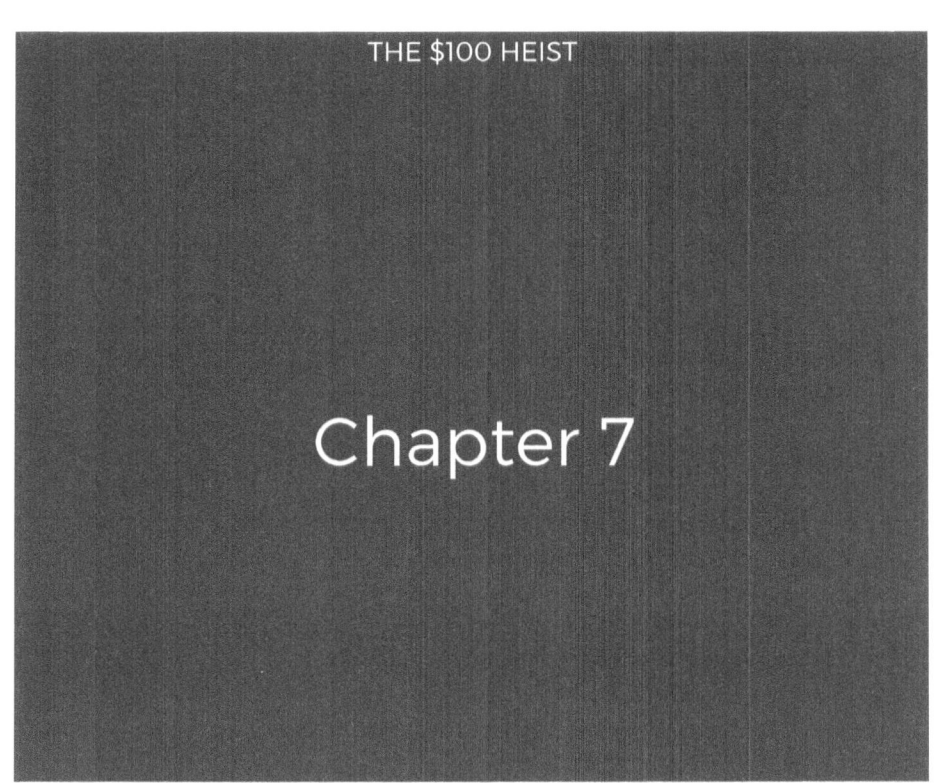

Chapter 7

The Magical Allignment of Buyers

The #1 Platform For Retailers—Facebook

Let me take you back in time... to 2011.

That might not seem like long ago, but you might be surprised to learn that in 2011 it was very difficult to make a profit with Facebook advertising. For some people, making a profit was downright impossible. I was one of the lucky ones. I was able to make several percentage points in profit from Facebook advertising.

Why was it so difficult? Back then, Facebook advertising was the new kid on the block. Even though Facebook had massive traffic, Facebook advertising was still in the very early stages of development. Many people didn't trust its validity or its viability.

Back then, I had come across a case study on an agency which handled the advertising campaigns of over a dozen automotive dealers around the U.S. One day, the founder received an email straight from the president of one of the companies that he worked for. This email put him into a state of shock. He actually felt offended by it.

The email subject line said, "Stop all Facebook Ads." He couldn't believe what he was seeing because he was making money for these people via Facebook advertisements and other traffic sources. Facebook was an integral part of the marketing campaign. This information led to a published article stating that General Motors had officially stopped advertising on Facebook. However, they did not specify why. In 2011 they were spending millions of dollars on Facebook and then they shut down their advertising campaign overnight.

Now, most people had no idea why General Motors stopped advertising on Facebook. But people in the marketing industry, like me, know for a fact that those ads were not working for them, even though Facebook advertising had huge potential.

Now, let's get into our time machine and come back to today. Since 2011, Facebook has made drastic changes to its advertising method. In fact, many automotive companies are now taking advantage of Facebook advertising. Not only is it much easier than other forms of advertising, but the ability to generate profit using Facebook is much greater than it was six years ago. Facebook now has over 2 billion active users worldwide. It's a massive network - the population of China!

Facebook can now do many things that even Google can't do. Right now, it is the only online advertising network that can compete with Google.

Why?

Because Facebook has one major capability that Google doesn't have: targeting!

Facebook spends a fortune to acquire the data they offer advertisers. Do you know why Facebook spent $11 billion on acquiring WhatsApp and Instagram - even though neither of these platforms was making money? You might think that it simply wanted to have more companies under its umbrella.

The truth is that Facebook wants to take advantage of all the WhatsApp and Instagram users who do not use Facebook. By using its Facebook data, WhatsApp data, Instagram data, and third-party data, Facebook can refine its targeting for advertisers like you and me.

What makes Facebook so massively huge right now - what allows entrepreneurs to make a fortune on Facebook - is its precise targeting ability. Seriously, what Facebook can do today in terms of precision targeting is unprecedented.

Let me give you an example. Let's say you have a yoga studio and you just hired a very handsome male yoga teacher. Before Facebook, if you were to advertise specifically for the classes taught by this handsome male instructor, you would have to place ads in the newspaper. You might also have created a Google ad, sent out flyers, or conducted a direct mail campaign.

But when you advertise in this way, you have no control over who sees your ad. If a man picked up that ad, he could easily toss it aside because he's simply not interested in yoga.

Your yoga studio needs to specifically target single women who are interested in yoga and who also live in the same general area as your studio. That's what Facebook allows you to do!

How? People comment, share, like, and put personal and geographic information in their profiles, and Facebook makes it possible for advertisers to take advantage of that data. This means your yoga studio can advertise specifically to females who are in the age range of 18 to 30, are single, live in your area, and love yoga.

This is what we call precision targeting. The chances that these people will click on your ad and sign up for classes grows exponentially because Facebook allows advertisers to fine-tune ads to ensure that the right people see them.

This kind of precision targeting is leading the way into a golden age of advertising. Right now, even beginners without any knowledge of advertising can, with very little guidance, profit from Facebook. Of course, you need the right knowledge and that is what I am going to share with you in the rest of this chapter.

On top of their precision targeting, what makes Facebook so successful is its pixel. A pixel is a piece of code that is installed into the advertiser's website. It is used to track the activities for the advertisers, providing real-time results on what is happening with the ads. It is used to measure ad performance. But if you take a deeper look at the technology, you'll find it does a lot more too.

With over 6 million active advertisers, Facebook has direct access to the activity on over 6 million websites. In this way, Facebook tracks every single click and behavior conducted on these websites to learn more about its users. It knows who will most likely purchase your product, who is somewhat likely, who is not likely, and who will absolutely not buy your product. Based on this data, Facebook shows your ads at the right time to the people most likely to actually buy. Leveraging this power gives you a major competitive advantage. That's why everyone flocks to Facebook when it comes to advertising online.

All in all, you need to know one thing: Facebook knows more about you than you know about yourself. As entrepreneurs, we need to leverage what is around us and use it to our full advantage. You need to master Facebook stalking. Yes, you need to stalk people on Facebook to turn them into buyers who will go to your e-commerce store and start buying products.

Stalking On Facebook

Let me make myself crystal clear: I am NOT teaching you how to stalk a beautiful woman on Facebook or how to spy on people on Facebook.

What I am about to describe is how you can use a piece of software that Facebook spent billions of dollars to create so that advertisers like you can actually stalk their buyers on Facebook. This software allows you to find out who they are, what they like, what their interests are, what their household income is, and what their behaviors are on Facebook.

Now, before I show you how to use this software, you need to come up with three important keywords that are related to your business.

First, find a keyword related to your niche. Let's say that you have a fitness e-commerce store. Your niche keyword is going to be one of the following: fitness, weight loss, or bodybuilding. These are your main keywords.

The second type of keyword is related to a public figure. You want to identify a key public figure in your niche. In fitness, one example is Jillian Michaels, but you can go to www.google.com and search for top public figures in fitness, and choose the one with whom you feel the most comfortable.

Your third keyword is a brand. You want to go after large, significant brands within your niche. In the fitness niche, one large brand is Beachbody. Another one is P90X. These brands are tailoring their messages toward the same niche as you.

How do you take advantage of this?

Once you have your three keywords, go to www.facebook.com/ads/audience-insights. Here you can see all the information about the audience that you want to target. Under Interests, on the left-hand side of the screen, you will type in each keyword, one at a time. You can start with body building, Jillian Michaels, or P90X.

When you enter Jillian Michaels, you will see that the demographic is 93% women. So, pretty much only women follow Jillian Michaels. You can also see that these are women are mostly between the ages of 25 and 34. Jillian Michaels' audience is mostly women; your ads need to be women-specific to reach and speak to these people.

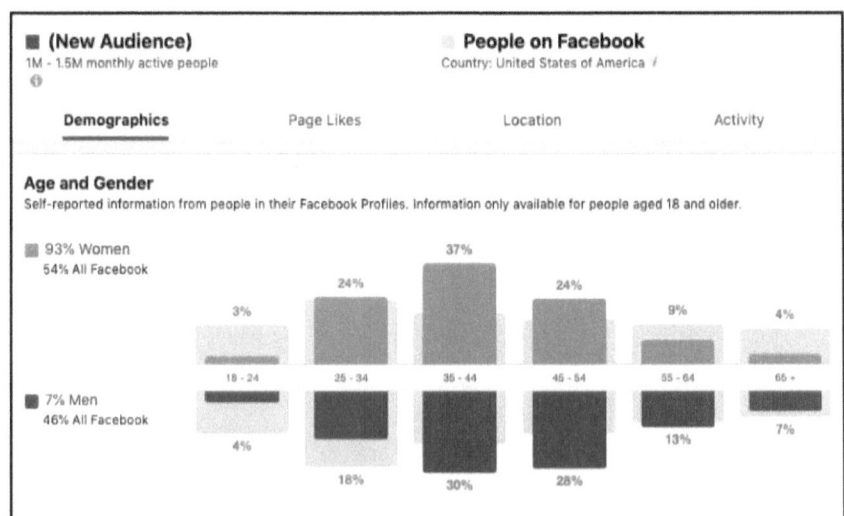

Now, if you look at the tabs near the top of the page, you will see Page Likes next to Demographics (the one you have been looking at). This will show you what your audience is interested in besides Jillian Michaels. This really has everything you need to really understand your market!

■ **(New Audience)** ■ **People on Facebook**
1M - 1.5M monthly active people Country: United States of America /
ⓘ

| Demographics | **Page Likes** | Location | Activity |

Top Categories

1	TV Programme	The Biggest Loser · This Is Us
2	Personal Blog	HIIT BURN
3	Coach	Trainer Lindsey
4	Food & drink	Eat - Fit - Fuel
5	Personal coach	Eat To Perform
6	Community	Hungry Girl · Fit Girls Guide · Crock Pot Girl · Scary Mommy
7	Product/Service	Beachbody · Fitbit · The Honest Company
8	Fitness Trainer	Burn20
9	Health & wellness website	The Betty Rocker · The Female Hardbody · MyFitnessPal
10	Public figure	Jillian Michaels · Bob Harper · Heidi Powell · Chalene Johnson · Chris Powell

See All

Another important tab to look under is **Activity**. Here, the most important thing to look at is **Ads Clicked**, which is the last column in the top graph. The grey compares the number of ads clicked to Facebook's entire database. The blue, which says 48 over 12, means that this audience is four times more likely to click on an ad. This is very important information!

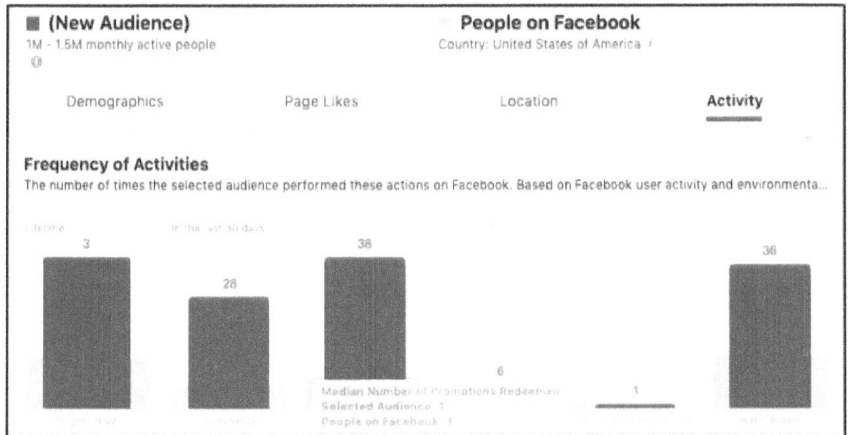

This is the beauty of Facebook!

This is how you can stalk your Facebook audience to understand who they are and what they like. Then you can craft the perfect message to these people, which will minimize your risk of spending that $5.

Skip that fancy drink at Starbucks tomorrow. Instead, you can have ads running on Facebook. But before we do that, let's define your first plan of action on Facebook.

Define Your First Plan of Action on Facebook

Now you know how to stalk your buyers on Facebook.

But you need to have a plan of action in place before you start advertising your specific message and your products to your audience.

First, you need to figure out what products you are going to advertise. It is very important for you to clearly understand which products work on Facebook - and which ones don't. Through my years in e-commerce, I learned the importance of finding themed products. This concept is critical for protecting you from losing money when advertising on Facebook.

What do I mean by themed products?

Themed products are products which fit a specific theme and can be tied to a very specific offer. A dolphin necklace is a themed product, and the theme is dolphins. Anyone who has expressed an interest in dolphins will likely buy that necklace.

It is critical to theme your products. The theme can be baby products, cats, nursing, or anything else. Let's use that butterfly watch as an example once again. I had never seen it before, yet I have sold hoards of them.

Now, if you do actually order a butterfly watch yourself to see what it looked like before you started selling them, you will discovered that it is the perfect product for Facebook advertising because you can advertise this product to people who have expressed an interest in both butterflies and watches.

We call this **Flex Targeting** and I will explain it in more detail in the next section.

However, the concept is essentially one that will minimize your risk of losing money while maximizing your results with Facebook advertising.

Now, remember that you will be offering the advertised product for freeplus-shipping. To find your products, go to AliExpress.com and look for niche products under the search function. When searching for products in your niche, you want to confirm two things before you decide to offer that product for freeplus-shipping.

First, as I mentioned in Chapter 5, make sure that the vendor has the option of ePacket shipping. This is very important! When a consumer buys something online, especially when it is the first time they interact with your store, you want to make sure they receive their product quickly. This won't be a problem if your vendors allow you to ship with ePacket.

Shipping			
Calculate your shipping cost by country/region and quantity			
Quantity: 1 Ship to: United States			
Shipping Company	Shipping Cost	Estimated Delivery Time	Tracking Information
POS Malaysia	US $0.00 Free Shipping	22-38 days	Not available
ePacket	US $2.44 US $1.45 You save: US $0.99 (about 41%)	12-20 days	Available
EMS	US $40.17 US $18.88 You save: US $21.29 (about 53%)	12-21 days	Available
DHL	US $52.54	6-13 days	Available

Second, make sure that the cost of your product, including the ePacket shipping, adds up to less than $5. This is extremely important when it comes to the free-plus-shipping model, because if you are charging $9.95 for shipping, then you will almost double the profit margin. This will ensure you can afford the advertising.

Once all this is established, all you need to do is find five to ten products to start.

Now, I'll be honest with you...

Not all of these products will make you money right away. However, if you can find even just one or two products that are profitable, you have instantly hit a home run. That's when you can increase your Facebook advertising budget and start making more money. The more products you offer for free-plus-shipping, the more money you will make. This is all based on quantity.

In Shopify, it's very simple. Once you have decided on a specific product you want to offer for free-plus-shipping, you need to add that product to your product page. Here is a template that will guide you through that process.

• The first paragraph will offer a detailed description of the product.

• The second paragraph will include a call to action (CTA): "Get this x, y, z product for free - just pay shipping and handling."

• Under the call to action, you need to say, "Please note: It will take 2 to 4 weeks for delivery." That way you are protected if a customer complains that their product hasn't arrived. You can say, "I told you up front that it would be 2 to 4 weeks for the delivery of your products."

Be sure to use the word **FREE!**

You must make sure you use the word FREE everywhere. You want it in your product title. You want it in your description, where you can use it and tell the customer they will pay just the shipping price.

Finally, before you hit Save, make sure the product is not part of any collection because you don't want your free products to be visible in your store. The reasons for this are twofold.

First, you want to create a sense of urgency. You want this offer to be very "special." If people go back to your store and see that everything else is free-plus-shipping, then they will lose confidence and no longer want to buy from you. You have one goal here: to create a buying frenzy! You want to let people know that they are getting a very special deal right now. You're basically saying, "If you go back to my store later, you won't find such a great deal."

The second reason you don't want your free products to be part of a collection is that eliminating the free products in your store forces your buyers to return to buy products at MSRP (manufacturer's suggested retail price). This provides you with a much higher profit margin. You thereby make more money because your customers are not just coming back for your free-plus-shipping stuff; they are actually coming back to buy other products. This is how you multiply what we call lifetime customer value and really sustain your long-term business.

Free plus shipping is not the only strategy that you can pursue to generate sales and profit for your store. Another big opportunity is selling products that solve a common problem. This is a massive territory offering lots of money to be made.

In any given niche, people have problems they want to solve. The solution might save them time or money, or simply make their life easier. Let's take the salad bowl below as an example.

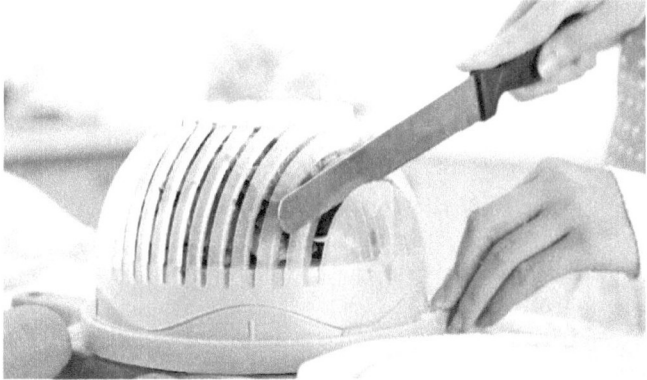

This simple product generated millions online because it solves a common problem: It saves time by slicing vegetables and fruit for salads.

When this product is showcased in a video demonstrating how it works, salad lovers buy it like hotcakes because the can see how much time they can save with it. It hits all the pain points and desire of the consumer.

Combine this desired solution with discounts and free shipping, and your sales will skyrocket. When you know your niche well, you can easily find this kind of product for your store and sell it by showcasing its benefit.

Writing the description for a product you are selling at a retail price isn't hard. Here's a quick template that you can follow:

• **First paragraph**: A story which tells the benefits of the product. Remember, never try to sell by focusing on a product's features. For selling a product at a retail price, you can also use bullet points in this first paragraph. For inspiration, check the product's Amazon listing. Amazon sellers are some of the best at writing benefit-focused bullet points. Mimic, but don't copy, the way these listings are worded.

• **Second paragraph**: Includes a call to action (CTA) such as "Get this x, y, z product for % discount." Include mention of FREE shipping if you offer that.

• **Under the CTA**: Include: "Please note: Allow 2 to 4 weeks for delivery. "That way you are protected if a customer complains that their product hasn't arrived. You can say, "I told you up front that it would be 2 to 4 weeks for the delivery of your products."

Once you have chosen your products and have everything in place, go to business.facebook.com and sign up for a Business Manager account. This is the platform from which you will place your advertising.

After you created your Business Manager account, go into Facebook, click on the navigation bar located on the top panel, and click **Pixels**. This is where you generate a pixel that can be installed on your website.

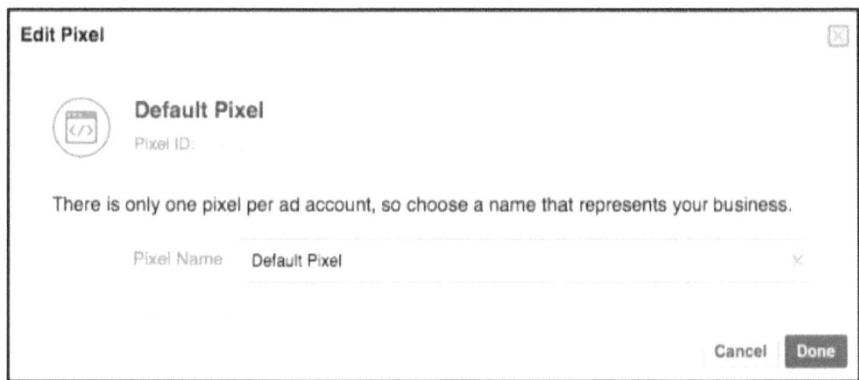

Look at highlighted section in the pixel screenshot below. This is a dedicated ID number for your account. You need to copy that ID number, go to your Shopify account, click on Sales Channel, then Online Store, and then Preferences. Here you will see a section that says Facebook pixel. Paste the ID number of your Facebook pixel here and click on Save.

When you do this, Facebook will help install your pixel on your website.

```
<!-- Facebook Pixel Code -->
<script>
!function(f,b,e,v,n,t,s){if(f.fbq)return;n=f.fbq=function(){n.callMethod?
n.callMethod.apply(n,arguments):n.queue.push(arguments)};if(!f._fbq)f._fbq=n;
n.push=n;n.loaded=!0;n.version='2.0';n.queue=[];t=b.createElement(e);t.async=!0;
t.src=v;s=b.getElementsByTagName(e)[0];s.parentNode.insertBefore(t,s)}(window,
document,'script','https://connect.facebook.net/en_US/fbevents.js');

fbq('init', '21724668          ');
fbq('track', "PageView");</script>
<noscript><img height="1" width="1" style="display:none"
src="https://www.facebook.com/tr?id=          &ev=PageView&noscript=1"
/></noscript>
<!-- End Facebook Pixel Code -->
```

Facebook Pixel

Facebook Pixel helps you create ad
campaigns to find new customers that look
most like your buyers. Learn more about
Facebook Pixel.

Facebook Pixel ID (how do I get this up?)

"But what's a pixel?" you may be asking.

Let me explain. In this golden age of internet advertising, we can do what cannot be done in traditional advertising. When you buy a newspaper ad, TV or radio commercial, or direct mail advertising, there is no way to know from where your sales are coming. It is always guesswork. That's why traditional advertising is not really an investment; it is an expense because you don't know whether or how you will get any monetary return.

With online advertising, the magic is in the pixel!

I shared some information about the Facebook pixel previously. Now let's drill down even more on this important topic. When you use pixels, Shopify actually tells Facebook exactly which ad resulted in the sale - and from which audience.

This makes it possible to optimize your ads. You can pause the ads that are not working and increase the budgets for the ones that are making you a profit because you receive accurate data that tells you precisely where you are making your sale.

Facebook has built its platform and their algorithm based on pixels. If you have pixels installed, you will allow Facebook to help you optimize your advertising campaign to make sure that you hit your objective: making sales!

The beauty of this system is that you are letting Facebook's multi-billion dollar software to do all the work for you! Facebook is helping you find the people who are most likely to buy products on your website. It does all the data analysis for you. For this reason, it is critical that you have your pixels installed.

Obviously, when you have the pixels installed, you still need to make sure you set up your Facebook ad correctly to maximize your ad message and increase your sales.

Now that you know the basics of Facebook's targeted advertising, I am going to show you the easy way to set up a Facebook ad. In fact, I am going to share with you one specific strategy that will minimize your risk of losing your money and increase your chances of making profits right from Facebook.

Facebook Ads—The Easy Way

I challenge you to log into Facebook right now and successfully run an advertising campaign. Chances are, you will be confused and not fully understand what needs to be done.

In fact, if you don't have any guidance, I can virtually guarantee you are going to lose money. My goal in this chapter is to make sure that doesn't happen. I will turn you into a master of Facebook advertising by minimizing your investment, maximizing your ad money, and maximizing your sales.

How can I do this? **By removing all the risk!**

I am going to share with you a step-by-step method that will provide you with what you need to minimize your risk of losing money with Facebook advertising. You might even hit the jackpot and start making profits almost instantly with an ad.

Do not try to reinvent the wheel. Trust me, I have spent millions on Facebook. I have a vast Facebook advertising experience and I know what works - and what doesn't. I have created a system that is super simple for anyone to copy.

All you have to do is bookmark this page, and whenever you set up a Facebook ad, simply follow what I am about to show you. You will minimize your chances of losing money while your chances of making money will increase dramatically.

Let's get to it.

The first thing you need to do is go back to business.facebook.com and click on **Create Ad,** located in the upper right-hand corner of the screen. You will be asked for your objective. There are over a dozen objectives from which to choose. You can ignore all of them except one, under Conversion, which is **increase conversions on your website.** You will choose this objective because you want to tell Facebook to help optimize your advertising campaign so you can make sure you increase sales.

That is all you care about. You just want sales. You don't want people commenting. You don't want people sharing. You don't want people liking your Facebook page. Of course, you do want clicks, but your ultimate goal is to increase sales on your website and you want to tell Facebook to focus on this.

So, under campaign objective, click **Conversions.** Then name your campaign based on the products you are selling and click **Continue.**

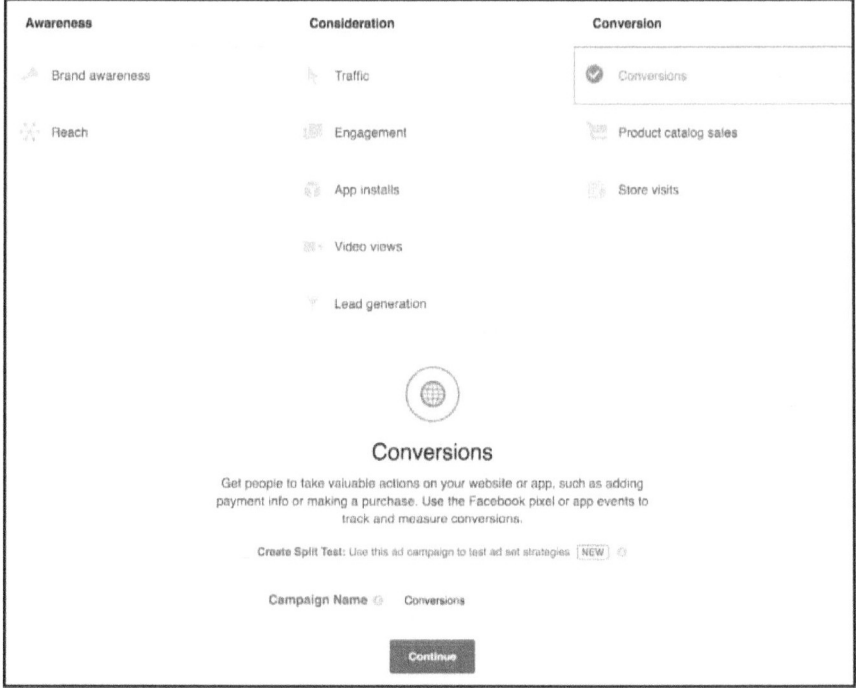

Next, you will be asked to choose a Conversion Event. Since we have utilized Shopify's easy integration of the Facebook pixel (discussed in the previous section), all you have to do is go to the **Conversion Event** drop-down menu and choose **Purchase.** This will tell Facebook that your goal is to make a sale.

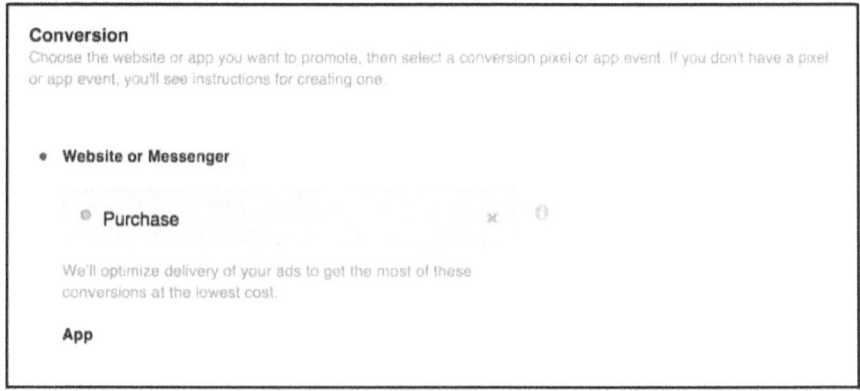

Note: Selecting the Purchase pixel is just for starters. As you grow your store and have more products to market, you'll want to create a specific purchase event pixel for each of the products you advertise. I will elaborate more later in this book.

Facebook now understands what you want. Facebook will use its pixel to track and measure the conversion and help you optimize your advertising to make sure that it is entirely based on the purchasing activity.

Next, under Audience, you absolutely must change the location to People who live in this location. If you leave it on the default Everyone in this location, anyone who goes there, even if they are just visiting, will see the ad. Since you are trying to sell a physical product to your audience and turn them into buyers, they must actually live in the area so that they can receive the product in the mail. They can't be traveling there from the UK, Australia, New Zealand, or China because that will affect the shipping cost.

So point to people who live in the location, and then choose people who live in that country or location. Eg : United States

Audience
Define who you want to see your ads. Learn more

Create New   Use a Saved Audience ▼

Custom Audiences   Add Custom Audiences or Lookalike Audiences

Exclude   Create New ▼

Locations   People who live in this location ▼

United States

⦿ **United States**

⦿ Include ▼   Type to add more locations   Browse

Add Bulk Locations...

Age   25 ▼ - 65+ ▼

Gender   **All**   Men   Women

Languages   **English (All)**

Another very important thing to consider is the age of the audience. Don't go after people who are under the age of 25. Start at **25 plus**.

True, at the age of 18 people will have a credit card, but let's be realistic. People between the ages of 18 and 25 often have a low credit card limits and they don't generally like to buy this kind of stuff online. In fact, if you have a product that works with the baby boomers, which is 45 and older, your chances of making a sale grow exponentially.

For one of my businesses, 90% of my sales are from 45 plus females. I can be super specific because I understand my audience. I know who they are. You, however, don't know who your audience is - yet. Facebook will provide you with the data so you will learn over time, but start with ages 25 to 65 plus for now.

That brings up the question of gender, which is optional. If you are selling fashion accessories, pet accessories, or any other female-dominated market, then you should check the **Women** option. In these cases, there is no point in targeting everyone, and there is no point in targeting just men.

However, if your products are ideal for both men and women, just leave **All** selected. Facebook then serves ads to both men and women and will track your results over time. If Facebook determines that more women are interacting with and buying from the ads, then it will automatically stop sending the ads to men and just send them to women. That's not a bad deal!

Next is **Languages**. A lot of people fail on Facebook simply because they leave this section blank, which will by default be set in the English setting if you're targeting the United States. Yes, it is true that everyone who lives in the United States understands English, but let's be realistic. In North America, we live in a multicultural society that consists of Indians, Pakistanis, Asians, Koreans, Japanese, Russians, and many other ethnic groups. Not all of them speak fluent English. So if you only want to target English-speaking people, enter in "English (All)" as your language to ensure that you are only targeting people who can understand English, thus people who can understand your ad that is written in English.

Imagine a person who has been living in Canada for the last 20 years, but her English is not good. She doesn't understand what an ad is saying if it's in English. So be sure that the language is not set blank. Many people log into their Facebook accounts in their own language. If they preset their Facebook account to be in a foreign language and you advertise in English, chances are very slim that you will succeed because they won't understand what your ad says.

Next, you need to look at Detailed Targeting. Pay close attention because this is where I'm really going to minimize your risk. You already know how to use Audience Interests to stalk your buyers.

Now I am going to share with you another strategy to minimize your risk: Flex Targeting. Take a look at the Venn diagram. The reason I am telling you to choose a themed product to advertise is so you can utilize this Venn diagram.

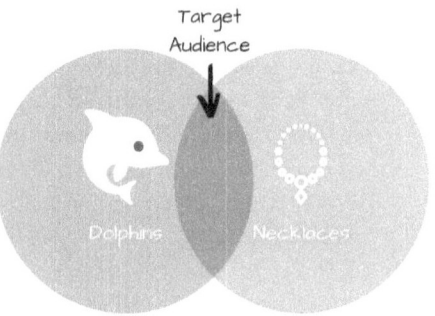

Let's say you are advertising a dolphin necklace. Obviously, you can send the ad out to anyone who is interested in dolphins. However, there are many reasons people might have an interest in dolphins, yet they have no interest whatsoever in a dolphin necklace. The truth is some people are forced into the dolphin detail targeting interest.

What do I mean by "forced into"?

Well, there will be people who are truly interested in dolphins, but there are also people in this audience who are what we call a forced like. You may very well have experienced this forced like yourself in the past.

If your best friend goes to Sea World and swims with the dolphins, that doesn't mean you love or even like dolphins. But since your best friend posted a photo of herself kissing a dolphin, you feel obligated to Like that post. Obviously, your Like of this post doesn't mean you are into dolphins. You might not want to be caught dead kissing a dolphin. But since you liked a post that was related to dolphins, Facebook will categorize you as having an interest in dolphins. When you Like the post, you are automatically put into the dolphin-interest pool!

You need to minimize the risk of targeting these forced likes!

How? By adding another layer of targeting. One circle on the Venn diagram represents dolphins and the second circle represents necklaces. The overlapping area in the diagram is your target audience because they like both dolphin and necklaces.

Do you see how this minimizes your risk?

You are selling a dolphin necklace and you are telling Facebook that you only want to send your ad to people who are interested in both dolphins and necklaces. This eliminates anyone that might like dolphins, but wouldn't buy a necklace. This strategy minimizes your risk because it dramatically increases your chances of making a sale. And it's very simple.

Simply go into **Detailed Targeting**, put the target keyword **dolphin** in Audience Interests and then click on **Narrow Further** below Detailed Targeting. Here you can add another keyword, which, in this example, is **necklace**. When you do this, you are literally forcing Facebook to **show ads to people who are interested in both dolphins and necklaces**. The audience the ad is shown to must match both words in order for it to work.

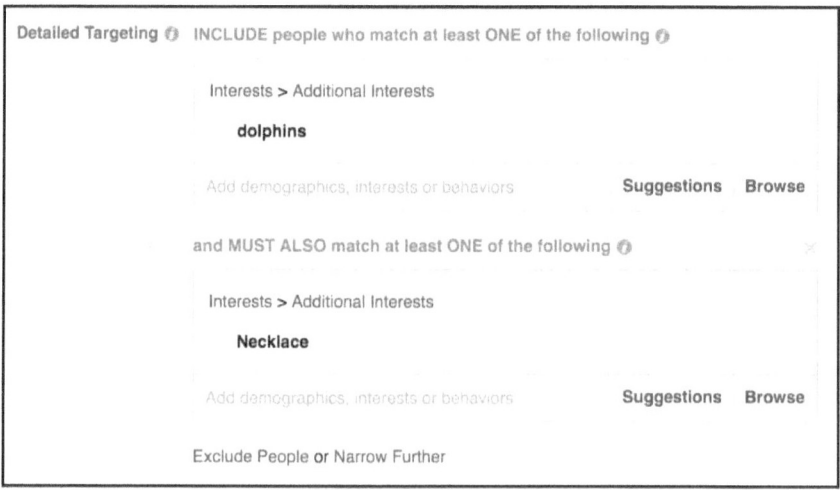

By doing this you are refining your audience; this will increase your chances of succeeding in this specific campaign.

Again, this is why the themed product works so well. If you are selling a cat product, such as a cat t-shirt, you can target people who like cats and people that express interest in tops, t-shirts, or hoodies. But be careful! Choose only one alternative interest. Don't go crazy adding a third or fourth interest. Doubling the interest overlay will accomplish what you need.

Another way you can use the Detail Targeting is starting off with what we call Precise Targeting. These are smaller groups of people, or people who have expressed an interest in a particular magazine. The audience size for this should hover around 300,000 and no higher than 1 million. Why should you start small? So that you can quickly determine whether the product will sell to a highly targeted audience before you spend more of your budget. If it doesn't sell to a small, targeted audience, then spending budget on a large audience will drown you in losses — not what we want.

So, remember: When you first go in market and you are not using Flex Targeting, start off with precise targeting with an audience size between 300,000 to one million maximum. If that's successful, then you can start to expand your audience targeting.

We are almost there, but we need to cover a little more.

Next, go to the **Placements** section. By default, this is set to run on **Automatic.** This means that your ads will be shown on mobile phones, on Instagram, and on Audience Network, which is Facebook's third-party ad server that shows ads on other websites via a mobile device. Your ad will also be shown on the Desktop Newsfeed, so people see these ads on their computers, and on the Desktop Right Column, which shows the ad in the right-hand column when looking through your newsfeed in Facebook.

For now, ignore all of these... except one!

Under Placements, click on the radio button next to **Edit Placements.** In the **Device Types** drop-down menu, select **Mobile Only.**

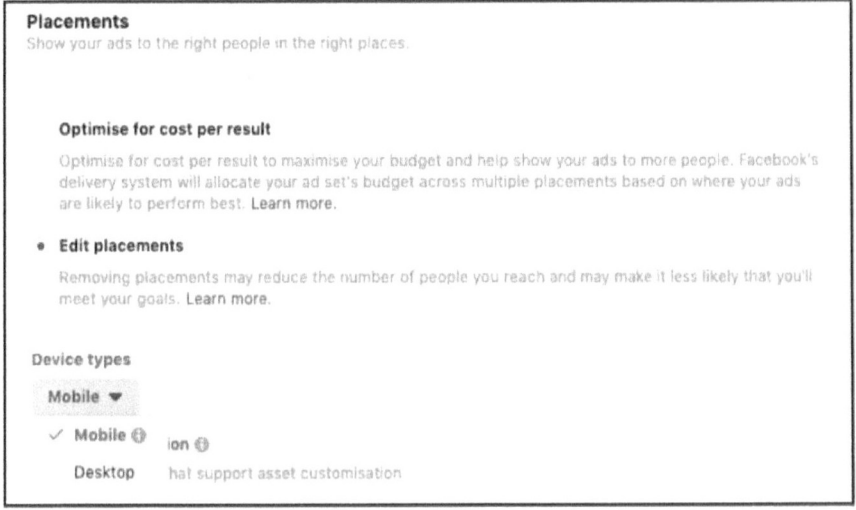

Then **uncheck Instagram and Audience Network** from the default platforms. Click on the little arrow next to Facebook and uncheck everything except Feeds. By doing so, **your ad will only target mobile users in their Facebook News Feeds.**

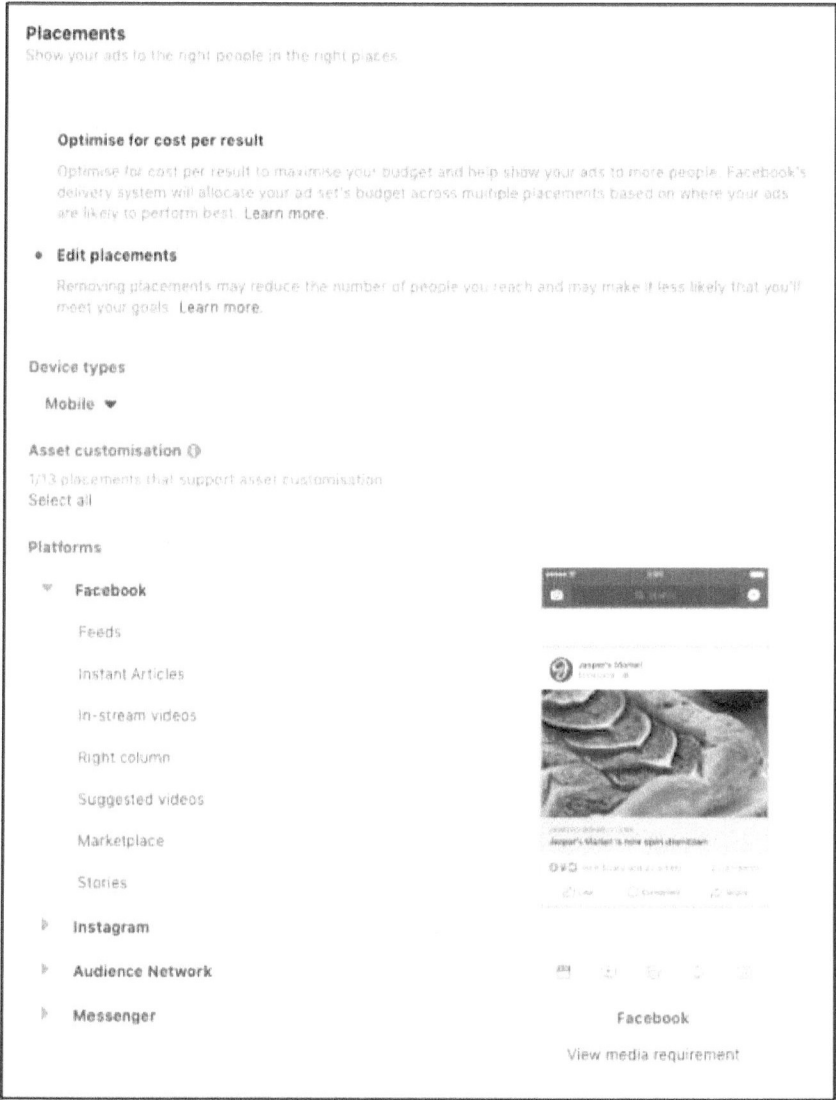

You might be surprised to know that almost every single e-commerce store on the internet right now is focusing primarily on mobile. In fact, a lot of online sales gurus will tell you to make sure you do mobile first because mobile is a much bigger market right now than desktop. Not only that but serving your ads on mobile will cost you much less than it will on desktop because the ad inventory on mobile is so much greater.

Now here is another very important point. At the very bottom of the Placements section under Advanced Options, click on the link that says "**Specific Mobile Devices & Operating Systems**".

ADVANCED OPTIONS
Specific Mobile Devices & Operating Systems
Exclude Categories for Audience Network
Apply Block Lists for Audience Network

In the Specific Mobile Devices & Operating Systems drop-down menu, make sure that it is set to All Mobile Devices. Then check the box next to "**Only when connected to-Wi-Fi**".

Specific mobile devices & operating systems

All mobile devices ▼

✓ Only when connected to Wi-Fi

Exclude content and publishers
Available for the Audience Network, Instant Articles and In-stream videos.

Apply block lists

Exclude categories ⓘ

Think about it. When people are on the go, whether they're waiting for someone, or the bus, or in the bank drive-thru lane, they usually have no Wi-Fi available - but they will most likely log into Facebook to check their newsfeed.

If they are on a 3G, LTE, or 4G network, then you know for a fact they are not going to spend a lot of time checking stuff on their phone. They are just trying to kill the 5 to 10 minutes they have, and that is not enough time to go through an entire buying process.

Simply put, people will not be checking out your product, buying it, and putting their credit card in place if they are not around Wi-Fi.

When people do have access to Wi-Fi, however, it usually means they are at home or work. If your ads are seen by people when they are at home, work, or another place where they have a chunk of extra time, then they are more likely to go through the buying process - and you have a better chance of making a sale.

Seriously. I can guarantee that if someone is on Wi-Fi, they are going to spend at least half an hour on their phone. But without Wi-Fi, they won't spend much time at all. So make sure you select Only when connected to Wi-Fi and you will have a great chance to increase your sales.

Next, you want to go to the Budget & Schedule section and choose a Daily Budget of up to $5. You don't need to spend $20, $100, or $1000. Just go with $5 and ignore everything else in this section. Next, click on Continue.

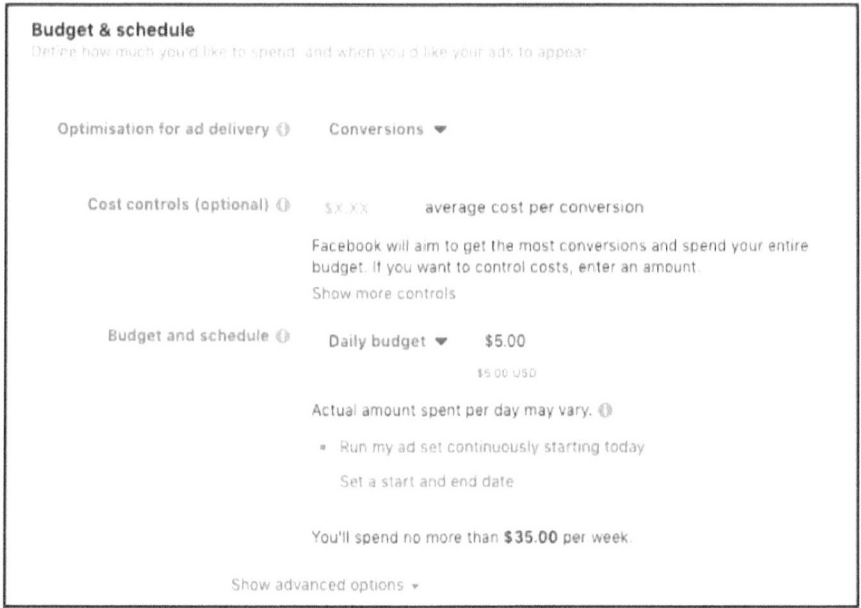

Now we come to the fun part: creating your ad!

When creating your ad, there are a few important factors and elements that you need to pay close attention to. Use this guide whenever you create an ad. I'll keep it as simple as possible, but I encourage you to read it several times. First, choose your Facebook Page from the drop-down menu.

Under the Format section you'll choose how your ad will look. There are 3 different formats that you want to fully utilize. We will start with an easy one first. Select Image or Video as your format.

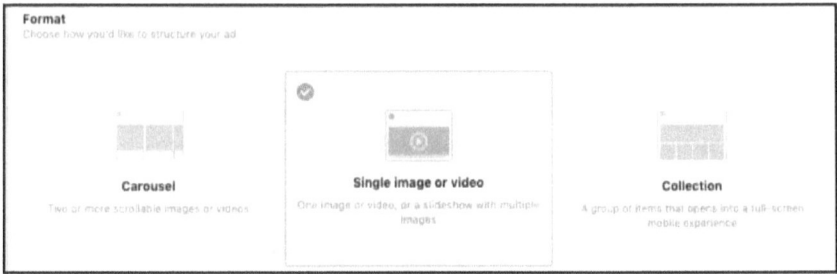

Now you'll be asked to upload the image that you want when you scroll down to the Media section. The recommended size for images used to be 1200 pixels by 628 pixels. However, as smartphone screens have evolved, Facebook now recommends a square image of 1080 pixels by 1080 pixels.

For the best image, go to AliExpress and locate your product's vendor. Download the product image or take a screenshot. The majority of photos on AliExpress are already in the shape of a square. If not, go to www.Canva.com to use the online web tool to resize the image to the square format of 1080 pixels by 1080 pixels. Remember to use a lifestyle image. Do not use images that simply display the product on a white background; it will not be attractive enough for your prospects to notice.

Once you have your image ready, simply upload it.

Next you will enter your website URL, and for this you want to copy and paste your product page. This ensures that when people click on your ad, they are taken directly to the product page where they can add the product to their cart and check out.

If you are using Tiny.ie, which I highly recommend, take your product page URL and shorten it inside Tiny.ie. Now enter the link which Tiny.ie generates into the website URL section. When we create your ad's text, you will learn how Tiny. ie can get more visitors to your website and reduce your Facebook advertising costs.

When you enter your URL, Facebook automatically pre-populates your ad's Headline and Text. However, you should change these to make your ad more attractive for people to click.

Free Plus Shipping Product Ads

If you are using the free plus shipping strategy, start your Headline with the word FREE followed by the product name. You should also change the Text to specifically trigger buying behavior. In essence, you want to create a YES right away.

People who teach sales techniques say the more times you get a "Yes" the greater your chance for closing the sale.So, going back to our trusty dolphin necklace example, we can start the text off by saying, "Love dolphins?" If the people are seeing this ad, then they expressed an interest in dolphins, and chances are, they love dolphins. When you say, "Love dolphins?" they will respond, "Yes, I love dolphins." Then you say, "Get this X, Y, Z product for free. Just pay shipping." Include a resonating emoji in your text to make your advertisement really stand out.

Text

Enter text that clearly tells people about what you're promoting

Website URL ⓘ   Preview URL

Enter the URL you want to promote

Build a URL parameter

Headline ⓘ

Call to action ⓘ
Learn More ▼

Multiple languages (optional) ⓘ
+ Create In Different Language

Hide advanced options ▲

Display link (optional) ⓘ

Enter the link as you want people to see it in your ad

News Feed link description ⓘ

That's it! Nothing fancy. Nothing crazy.

My Perfect Facebook Ad Template

If you're not using the free plus shipping strategy, then you will need a different kind of text to attract people to click and become customers. I call this my Perfect Facebook Ad Template for e-commerce. It's based on the proven effective AIDA formula.

AIDA is a long-proven selling model used in all kinds of industries to describe the effects of advertising on prospects from their first exposure to an ad to the decision to purchase. The AIDA acronym stands for:

Attention
Interest
Desire
Action

Attention. Getting attention for your ad is very important; without it, your prospect will not even see the rest of your ad. But studies have shown that human beings have lower attention spans than goldfish. And with advertising, our attention spans are even shorter: You have less than 3 seconds to capture the attention of the prospect with your ad.

To get attention for your ad, use no more than 6 words. These 6 words must grab the person's attention with a "hook" — an angle that hooks the person in.

For example, let's say you are selling a stainless steel dumpling maker to people who are interested in dumplings and in recipes. To capture your audience's attention, your ad hook could be "Make The Perfect Dumpling In Seconds." This immediately hooks the person in to pay attention the advertisement. To help the hook stand out even more, add one or two related emojis at the front and back.

Interest. Now that you've got the prospect's attention, you need to get them interested in your product. In one to two sentences max, you need to showcase the product benefit to get your prospects interested. Remember, consumers do not care about features. They only care about benefits.

For example, do you know the horsepower of your car? Probably not. You only care about your driving experience. Now, there are some small exceptions to this rule. One way that I write the Interest section is to put yourself in your prospect's shoes and answer the question, "What's in it for me?" Put the answer in this section and your ad will produce higher results.

Desire. By now you have shifted the person's mind to your product. Your next task is to get them to desire your product. Here it's important to remember that consumers buy based on wants, not needs. To get that desire, present them an irresistible offer. Tell your prospects either the product is free, or it's at a massive discount, or it's shipped free. This will make the person want the product because they don't want to miss out on the deal.

Action. This simple step is overlooked by many advertisers because it seems too obvious: telling people specifically what to do. People loved to be told exactly what to do even when it's a given. Say, "Grab this deal now," "Shop now," "Buy now," or "Get yours today." Then add an arrow emoji pointing to your website URL. This little trick will instantly increase your clicks and visitors.

Keep in mind that a long product page URL will mess up the look of your ad. This is why I recommend Tiny.ie's shortened link to make your ad look clean and appealing. Facebook automatically underlines your URL to show it's a hyperlink. This also helps get more clicks because most internet users are trained to click underlined links to land on the desired page.

Now that you've written the text portion of your ad, let's move to the **Headline** section. Here, I usually expand on the original hook, as this area can have more characters. I also add several emojis in the beginning to capture the person's attention as well.

Then go to **Call To Action** and select Shop Now. You are essentially programming these people, telling them to shop now, and that they need to buy something now. You can then go to the **News Feed Link** Description, where you want to put in additional text for the product. You can say, "Limited-Time Offer Only. Grab Yours Now."

Then simply click **Place Order** at the bottom of the page, and you are done!

Congratulations! You have now mastered my Perfect Facebook Ad Template. I use this for all my advertisements on Facebook and all of my students' ads as well. We have torture-tested this format and it is proven to produce the highest results. This method alone will pay for the investment you made in this book

What I've shared with you so far is the simple version of getting traffic to your product page using a Facebook ad. But I don't want to only share the basics. I want to share ALL my secrets. I want to empower you with all the knowledge you need to become successful just by investing in this book.

That said, let's move to a more advanced version of the Facebook Ads setup. I'll also show you the strategy that my students and I use to rapid-fire our testing to quickly find that revenue producing product.

3X3 Facebook Ad Formula

Throughout my years of buying traffic online, and as a media buyer, I've noticed that I do something unique each time I test a new product or campaign. To attract different audiences, I use different messaging to see what sticks. When I first started sharing this technique, it was confusing and hard to explain.

So I invented my 3x3 Ad Formula.

If you look at the diagram below, you'll notice that with the easy way, we only created one leg of the 3x3 Ad Formula. But to make the right decisions on your e-commerce store's product advertising, you'll want to complete the entire 3x3 Ad Formula to rapid-fire test and get results.

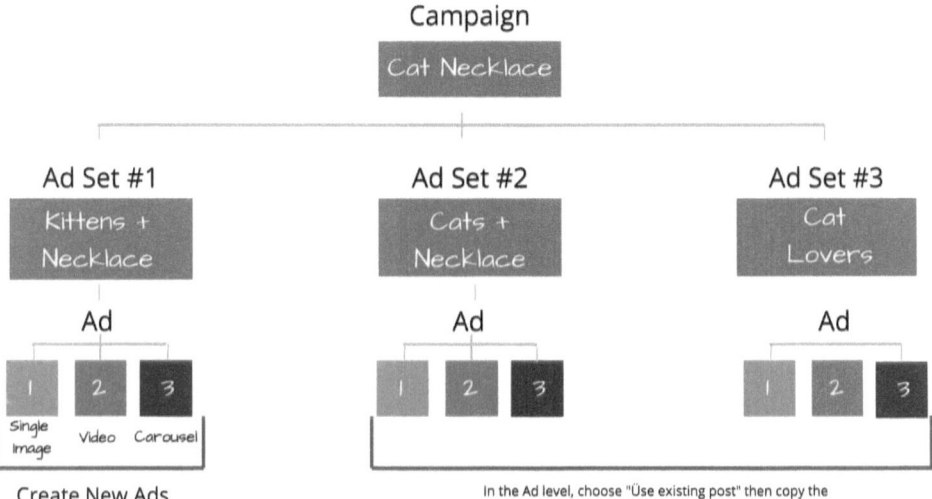

One main reason why this 3x3 Ad Formula is crucial is its ability to quickly narrow down what is working and what is not working for your business. In e-commerce, three main factors will make or break your bank: Product, Targeting, and Message.

The 3x3 Ad Formula quickly gives you this crucial information. For every product you want to sell and advertise, you want to create one singular campaign. This campaign's sole purpose is to sell the one product. This is why at the top you'll see that the campaign is equal to your product.

Right under your campaign, you should have 3 different ad sets. These 3 different ad sets target and attract 3 different types of potential customers.

Last, we have 3 different messages or advertisements under each of the 3 ad sets. This forms the 3x3 Ad Formula. In only 24 to 48 hours, you will immediately know if it is the Product, the Targeting, or the Message that's working or not working. Let's get it implemented for your store.

If you have already gone through the easy way of setting up your Facebook Ads, you will have completed the first leg. We want to complete the full ad set with three different Messages and Ads first, before we complete the rest. With the rest, I'll share a quick technique that only requires a few minutes of your time.

Go into your Facebook Ads Manager (where you created your first campaign) and click on the Campaign Name that you have set. Then, you will be brought to the Ad Set level. Click on the Ad Set and you will be brought to the Ad Level. This is where you want to create the remaining two Messages and Ads. Since we have already created an Image ad, the next two are going to be Videos and Carousels.

Carousel Ad

Let's start with a Carousel ad first. A Carousel ad is used to tell a story to your customers through images or videos in a single advertisement. Your customers can engage and interact with the ad to view different images or videos. A Carousel ad is used to showcase different benefits of your product and shows your product from a different perspective.

To create your first Carousel Ad, click on the green **Create Ad** button. You will be brought to the Create Ad screen you saw earlier when creating your Image ad. This time, instead of selecting the Format as Image Or Video, select **Carousel**. You will see a slight difference in the setup than what you did with the Image Ad setup, but most is the same.

First, fill in the Text section the way you did with the Image Ad. You can copy exactly the same Text you used before, or create different messaging. It's entirely up to you. I'm lazy so I use the same Text to maximize the Carousel function instead. Next, leave the two section checkboxes as checked by default.

Now onto the Cards. These are basically where your customers can interact and view different images of your product. Find two more images from your vendor showing the product from a different perspective. Upload them with a different Headline in each to elaborate on the hook and the image itself.

Last, the destination URL is simply the product page URL or the Tiny.ie URL. Use the same URL under the See More URL as well. Then, as in the Image Ad, select the Call To Action to Shop Now. Finally, click on the green Confirm button and publish your Carousel ad.

Video Ad

To complete the full ad set, we need to now create a Video ad. The Video ad is the most commonly used ad format in Facebook. For e-commerce, the Video ad is vital for selling products. But you may be wondering, "I don't have the product with me. How can I create a video with it?" The answer lies in what I'm about to tell you.

What I'm about to tell you, completely changed the way we run our Facebook Video ads. We no longer need to record a video to start a Video ad!

Well, at Facebook they call this solution a **ThumbStopping** ad. The majority of people use a mobile device to scroll through Facebook and Instagram. When they see something attractive, they stop scrolling with their thumbs. This is why it is called a Thumb-Stopping ad. Since the motion of a video is usually what stops thumbs, the main purpose of a Thumb-Stopping ad is to help advertisers easily turn their still images into a video.

I felt something was missing when I was being introduced to the ThumbStopping ad: the AIDA formula. But I was wrong. It's easy to combine AIDA with a Thumb-Stopping ad. And once I did, my cost per visitor drastically dropped and my ads became way more engaging.

Creating a Thumb-Stopping ad is easy. All you need is the **Quik - by Go Pro smartphone app**. It is 100% free. You can get it on the App Store if you are using an Apple device and at the Google Play store if you are using an Android.

Once you download the app, go to AliExpress.com on your mobile phone, find the product you are selling and download the images. I always aim for 6 different photos and remember to use lifestyle photos. If you don't have enough photos, go to PixaBay.com to download images related to your product. Then open up the Quik app and select all 6 of the photos.

Now you get to select the motion template for the way you want the images to be shown. On the next tab which looks like a music icon, select the background music that fits what you are selling.

Next, go to the middle tab to enter text on top of your image. This is where your AIDA formula comes in. The first image should have your hook text. The second and third image should have your Interest text. The fourth image should have your Desire text. The last photo should have your call to action. Save the video and you are all set. Now you have your Thumb-Stopping Video!

Now repeat the process just like the Carousel above. This time, select Image or Videos, enter the same text you used for your Image Ad, and you're all set. This should fully complete the first ad set with 3 ads in each. Now, it's time to finish the entire 3x3 Ad Formula.

Go back to the campaign level, select your campaign, and you'll be in the Ad Set level. Click Duplicate under your Ad Set Name and you'll see a pop-up window. Select Existing Campaign and choose the campaign you want this ad set to be duplicated to. Then click Duplicate.

Now you will be brought to the Ad Set section where you will want to change the Detailed Targeting to a different target audience. Then click on the green Publish button.

Repeat this process one more time with a different target audience.

 You have now fully completed the 3x3 Ad Formula!

Regardless whether you are running the easy way or my 3x3 Ad Formula, let your ad run overnight so you have data to start analyzing and optimizing its performance. However, before analyzing your data, you need to understand your customer's journey first.

Understanding The Psychology of Your Customer's Journey

Most businesses and e-commerce store owners overlook the psychology behind the customer's journey. You may have the best product, the best price and even the most beautifully designed website. But without knowing and understanding the psychological behavior of your customers, you will be leaving money on the table.

As an entrepreneur, you need to know what happens from the first point of interaction with your customers all the way to the very end when you receive money from your customers. Knowing this information is powerful and will allow you to optimize your business effectively. Combine this with the data that you receive from your advertising investment, and you'll find that a simple tweak can make a drastic impact to your bottom line.

Let's first look at the customer's journey using the diagram below:

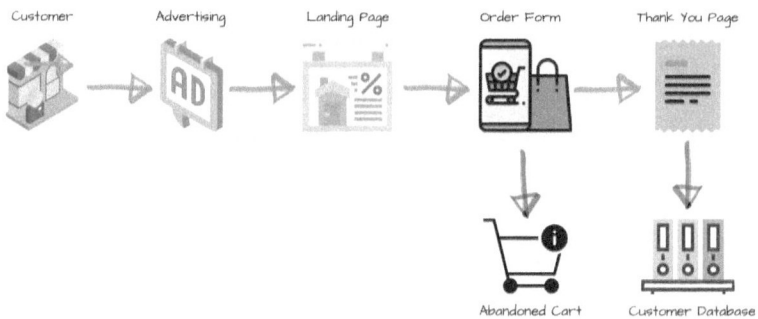

The first interaction your potential customer has with you is your advertisement. The ad itself narrows down who's interested in your product.

Remember, people do not randomly click on an ad or a post. They click for a reason: They want to learn more about your product and your offer. When they click your ad, they're giving you their first "Yes I want this product" trigger so you can then continue to sell them.

When your potential customers click on your ad, they land on your product page — your landing page. On this page, your job is to sell them the product by telling a story and talking about the product benefits. These page visitors are fully aware of what you are selling. Now your job is to simply close the deal.

On this landing page, one of two possible results will occur regardless of your pricing strategy. One result may be that your potential customer adds the product to the shopping cart. This is your ultimate goal. The second possible result is that the customer leaves your page without adding the product to the cart.

People leave for two reasons. First is that the price is higher than they expected. Second is that the benefits of the product are not enticing enough. If you are selling the product for a set price and people leave, it's definitely the price that is stopping them from moving forward. Simply drop the price of the product and you'll start seeing add to carts happening. Again, your goal on this page is to trigger the add to carts.

The next two steps of the customer's journey is the process of entering their information details. The beauty of Shopify's checkout process is that once people add the product to the cart and initiate checkout, they need to enter all their information before they see the shipping price. This lets you collect customer information even if they abandon the cart. This is why having the Abandonment Protector app is vital — so you can set up emails to remind customers to come back to finish their transaction.

During the checkout process, it is normal for people to abandon the cart. In fact, 66% of consumers leave the cart due to various reasons. Most of the time it is the shipping price that makes people abandon the cart. If you are experiencing a high number of add to carts but you have not yet generated a sale, it may be that your shipping fee is stopping your customer. This is clearly demonstrated when you are using the free plus shipping model.

On the other hand, if you offer free shipping and your customers still abandon the cart, there are two things you can do: You can retarget them with anadvertisement (I'll talk about this later in this book). You can also simply set up Abandonment Protector emails to remind them to finish the transaction.

Now that you know the customer's journey and the reasons why they may have left during the buying process, let's move into data. This data will make it easy for you to make the right decisions on how to optimize your advertising.

Interpreting The Data To Find Your Jackpot

Let data tell you the story. I cannot stress the importance of this enough. If you don't let data tell you what is happening, you leave yourself at risk of losing more money than you want, or of leaving easily-grabbed money on the table.

We are living in the best time in history when it comes to advertising online. We get real-time data that allows us to make the right decisions. If you ignore the data, it will affect your business.

Using the right data, backed by my 4 Levels Of Optimization system, you will spend far less money figuring out whether you have a winning campaign or a losing campaign.

Now, as much as I dislike saying it, Facebook's default ad reporting is quite misleading. A wealth of key information is not shown unless you customize your reporting to show it. To make the right decisions, you need the following information to fully understand what is happening with your advertisements and with your customer's journey.

CPC (Cost Per Click) Link: How much you pay per click for someone to go to your website.

CTR (Click-Thru-Rate) Link: A percentage calculation demonstrating the rate of clicks on your advertisement.

Cost Per Purchase: How much you pay to acquire one sale.

CPM (Cost Per Thousand Impression): How much you pay for every 1,000 times your advertisement is seen.

Add To Cart: How many people added your product to the shopping cart.

ROAS: Return On Ads Spend. It's a KPI (Key Performance Indicator) to tell you how much return you have from your ad spend. 1.0 means that for every $1 you advertise, you make $1 back.

There are a few more data points that can help you make better decisions, but the ones listed above are enough to make informed decisions from your advertisement. To get these items to appear in your Facebook ads reporting, first log in to your Facebook Ads Manager. Then on the middle of the page, right above your data table, click the Columns button. Then click Performance and Clicks. This will give you a number of other data points that you might want to see, but it is still missing the key ones I mentioned above.

Now, click on the Columns button again, and this time click Customize Column. Now you will see a window that pops up to allow you to choose other metrics you want on your dashboard. In this window, select: Add To Cart Total, Purchases Cost, and Purchase ROAS. Last, check the box that says Save as Preset on the left-hand corner, and give it a name. This will save your customized report so you do not have to repeat this process each time.

Now that you've got your data and metrics, it's time to start analyzing and optimizing your store. Next, calculate your CPA (Cost Per Acquisition). Your CPA should be the break-even point of your product. Let's say that if you are selling a Garlic Grinder which costs you $5.20 to be shipped to your customer, and you are selling it for $19.95. Take $19.95 minus $5.20. This equals $14.75. The $14.75 is your desired CPA; you want to optimize your advertisements based on $14.75.

The 4 Levels of Optimization System

With the CPA calculated, use my 4 Levels Of Optimization to optimize your advertisement 24 hours, 48 hours, and 72 hours after you have started your ads. Take a look at the diagram below and I'll explain.

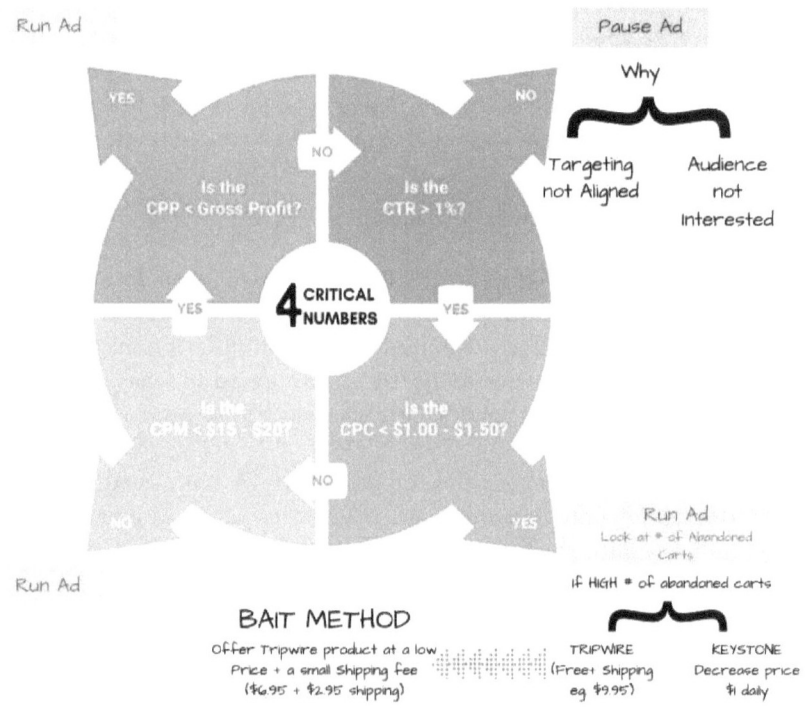

Optimization Level 1

The first level of optimization is to look at your Cost Per Purchase. Did you get a sale? If you did and your Cost Per Purchase is under $14.75, then continue to run the ad for another day. However, if you did not get a sale, move on to the second level of optimization.

Optimization Level 2

In the second level of optimization, you look at the CTR (Link). The CTR (Link) tells you if your product and message is resonating with your potential audience or not. If your CTR (Link) is under 1.00%, then immediately pause the ad. Why? Because without even looking at the other levels of optimization, we know that your audience is not interested in your product.

However, if your CTR (Link) is above 1.00%, then move on to the third level. Before we move on to the third level, be aware that your CTR should aim for 3.00% or higher. You achieve this by selling the product with a great benefit and an offer that is irresistible to the audience.

Optimization Level 3

Look at the CPC (Link). Is your CPC (Link) lower than $1.50? (It's best for this number to be lower than $1.00.) If it is, then look at the number of Add To Carts. Since you are experiencing a high CTR (Link) and a low CPC (Link), it means that your audience is interested in what you have to sell but something is not right in your customer's journey.

This is why you want to look at your Add To Carts next. The following metric applies only to products that you are selling at a set retail price. If you are not getting any Add To Carts, then it means that you priced your product too high and your audience is not seeing the perceived value of the product. If this is the case, drop the product price until you start seeing Add To Carts which will eventually lead you to your first sale.

If you are getting a good number of Add To Carts but you are not getting any sales and you are selling the product at a retail price, then you are probably charging shipping. Remove the shipping fee if you have enough margin to do so and you will start seeing sales roll in.

If you are using a free plus shipping strategy and getting a high number of Add To Carts — but no sales — then the customer cannot justify the perceived value to be $9.95 (the magic number you need for free plus shipping).

In this case, switch to the Bait Method. With the Bait Method, instead of charging $9.95, price the product at $6.95 plus $2.95 shipping. Mathematically, the total price is the same. But you have shifted the psychology of the customers to lead them to believe it's only $6.95.

What if your CPC (Link) is higher than $1.50? Chances are you should pause the advertisement because it's impossible for you to make a profit or break even with such a high CPC (Link). Again, your goal is $1.50 or lower (or better, $1.00 or lower). But before you pause this ad, look at the last level of optimization.

Optimization Level 4

The fourth level of optimization is your CPM. You want to get into a market with a CPM around $15 to $20 if you are not achieving the 3 levels of optimization above. If your CPM is higher than $20, that means your market is pretty competitive. If you are not achieving the 3 levels of optimization mentioned, it's basically telling you to stop the ad or even drop the product altogether.

With the 4 Levels Of Optimization system, you may want to make tweaks and adjustments. Look at which ad is performing best, and at which ad set is performing the best. Pause the ones that are not in alignment with the 4 Levels of Optimization. Continue running those that are in alignment with the numbers mentioned above.

If by now you have generated your first sale, congratulations! If you haven't, don't worry. Your first sale will come. You just need to continue to find more products, create more ads, use the data to tell you what is happening, and make the necessary adjustments needed.

The #1 Advertising Trick That Lifted Amazon's Sales

There's never a 100% conversion rate. What do I mean? You will never be able to get 100 visitors to your website and have all 100 of them buy your product. This virtually impossible. There is, however, an advertising trick that Amazon knows. In fact, Amazon has fully exploited this #1 advertising trick to generate huge revenue for their business.

A large number of people will express interest in your product and even start your customer journey — without buying. We call these people "warm traffic." Warm traffic is the lowest-hanging fruit for your business.

When you shop on Amazon and browse through products, you don't purchase everything you see every time. You decide that you might buy later. But the minute you leave Amazon, the very same product that you were viewing continues to follow you on Facebook… until you finally give in and end up buying the product. This strategy is called Dynamic Retargeting and you can easily implement it for your business.

Retargeting is one of the most advanced technologies in online advertising. But how does it actually work?

When a prospect visits your website, a cookie is automatically installed onto that person's computer through the website's pixel. Through this cookie, the pixel tracks every behavior and event including whether the visitor bought a product from you or not. It then sends this information back to the advertising platform. When your customers go to your website but don't buy anything, they are put into a pool of audiences to whom you can target with a specific ad message on Facebook until they buy.

Now the Dynamic part comes in, based on the product your visitor was viewing in your store. You get to advertise only to those who went to your website, and the ad they see is exactly the product they were checking out. This is one of the most powerful methods of advertising and offers the highest ROI (return on investment) of any advertising you can do.

To do this, some technical work needs to be done. First, you will need an app like Pixel Bay. With Pixel Bay, you can create a catalog of products within your Shopify store and sync it up with your Facebook Ad account. To do this, go to the App Store and get Pixel Bay. It'll cost you $9 a month but it's totally worth it. (This app offers more features than dynamic retargeting. I'll explain later in this book why I recommend Pixel Bay.)

Once you've got Pixel Bay, head over to the Settings Tab and Connect Your Facebook Account. After you have connected your Facebook Account, head back to Settings. From the drop-down menu, choose the Facebook Ad Account that you are using for your ads and hit Save. Now, right under the drop-down menu, you will see the RSS Feed URL. Copy that RSS Feed URL to a notepad.

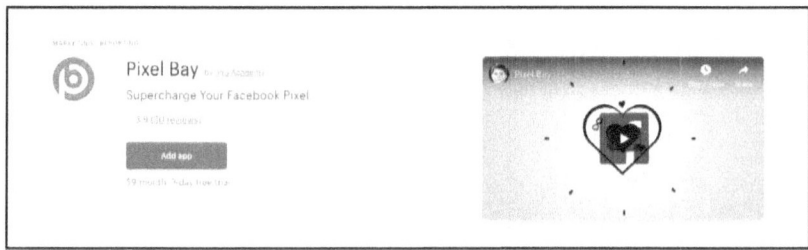

Next, head over to your Facebook Ads Account and go to the main menu on the top left. Under Assets, click **Catalogs**. Click the big blue button that says **Create Catalog**. Select E-commerce. Select Upload Product Info. Give your catalog a name and click the big button again.

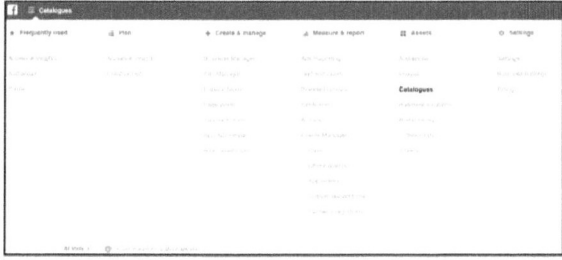

Now go to the left-hand menu and click **Product Data Sources**. Add Data Sources on the right-hand side, and then click Use Data Feeds.

Then, under "How do you want to upload your data feed?" click **Set a Schedule**. Paste the RSS Feed URL you copied from Pixel Bay and paste it under the Data Feed URL. Schedule it to Hourly and click **Start Upload**. Once the upload has been completed, the last step is to connect your Facebook Pixel. Head over to the Settings on the left-hand menu and click **Connect Event Source**. Select your Facebook Pixel for your Facebook Ads account and you're done!

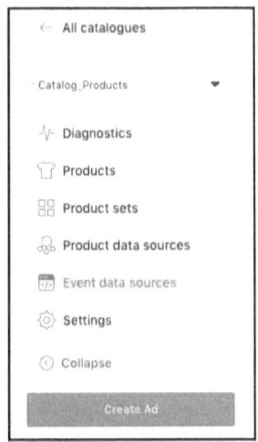

Now that you've got the setup completed, you need to create your Dynamic Retargeting ad. Go back to your Facebook Ads Manager and click the **Create** button. This time, instead of choosing Conversions, choose Catalog Sales. Name your campaign and select your catalog from the drop-down menu. Click **Continue**.

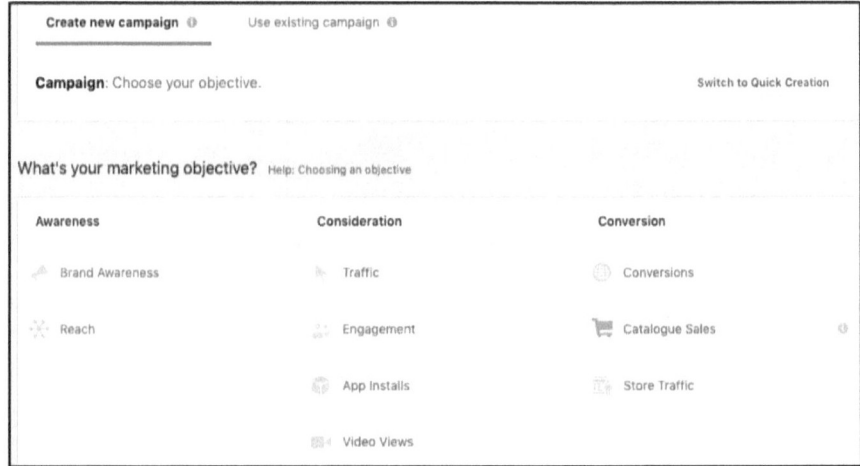

Now on the Ad Set creation, I suggest you leave everything as default and simply enter whatever budget you desire. The default setup will already be set up to retarget your ad to those who visited your website, or added a product to cart in the last 14 days but didn't purchase from you.

Click **Continue to Ad Level**. On the Ad Level, select your Facebook Page and use the Carousel Format. Then all you need to do here is fill in the Post Text, add some emojis, and you are all set. For the Post Text, I usually acknowledge that the customer visited my website but left for some reason, and I offer a coupon to come back to purchase the product. Basically, I'm offering the "What's in it for me?" answer so that they return to my website and complete the purchase.

Now you're all set up with the same advertising strategy that Amazon uses! You will see the best ROI using this strategy. Dynamic Retargeting maximizes your investment when advertising your products on Facebook or any other platform.

Chapter 8

The Million Dollars

Scale Up. Whale Up!

I think one of the most frustrating things for a business owner is hitting a sales ceiling.

I know this because it happened to me. For three years in a row, every one of my businesses was hitting a ceiling that I simply couldn't get past.

I was stuck. I wanted to build my businesses past the $10 million mark, but it was much harder than I expected. My personal goal was to surpass $10 million.

I was moving forward, but it was going very slowly!

I was afraid of this plateau, so I took a long, hard look at my system. It was then that I realized that my system was missing something. It was missing a very critical step. I realized that I had been doing something very wrong. I certainly was not using one specific method to multiply my business in a big way. I felt like I had been hit by a bus. I realized right then and there that I had been leaving a ton of money on the table.

I wasn't emailing my clients. I wasn't doing any product launches. I was just focusing on the first three steps of my system: building and maintaining my e-commerce store, leveraging inventory arbitrage, and generating traffic.

At that point I had a brand and I had traffic, but I was missing what we call a "backend." No, I'm not talking about my own personal backend! In business, the backend is basically a method of magnifying or multiplying your business whenever a customer walks through your online door. I call it the profit multiplier - and it is the lowest hanging fruit of my entire 5-Step Framework.

Scaling Up with Emails

Are you ready for this?

The profit multiplier has just three steps. That's all. Just three simple steps that you need to take in order to maximize your backend.

Step number one is emails. Yes, just emails. I can tell you with 100% honesty that by simply applying emails to my business, I created an additional stream of income and boosted my business by 20%.

Think of this in the proper scale. When you are running a seven-figure business, 20% is a massive amount of money to add because of something so very easy. Sending out emails doesn't cost you money and it's incredibly simple. So it is critical that you maximize your client database in this way, simply asking them for more sales.

Step number two is average order value. This is the average amount people spend on one purchase at your store. To generate more profits, you want to have your customers spend the most money possible in one single transaction.

Step number three is diversification. This means coming up with new products and new product lines. If you do not change in this way, you will be left behind. You absolutely must diversify!

When I applied these steps, my business was transformed. When I diversified my products, wrapped this diversification around a product launch, increased my average order value, and used emails, my business skyrocketed.

These three steps literally doubled my business. All I had to do was apply the profit multiplier. In fact, as I diversify my products, I am actually slowly moving away from being a re-seller of well-known products using inventory arbitrage, and instead creating my own products under my own brand.

But before I talk about the steps you need to take to diversify your e-commerce store, I want to make you a master at sending emails. Using email as a marketing tool is not quite as easy as it looks! That's why I am now going to make sure you know exactly how to use emails to increase your sales almost overnight.

Sending emails might look simple, but if you don't have the right resources and the right knowledge, you will fail. When it comes to e-commerce, you are not simply sending an email like you would to a friend. No, the emails you send via your business are what you use to broadcast a message to your entire database of customers.

In order for you to broadcast your message, you need to make sure you have the right software. That's right. Your Gmail account isn't going to cut it. The software has to be incredibly versatile and reliable. Fortunately, there are many options on the market right now, such as MailChimp, AWeber, GetResponse, and Infusionsoft. Each one of these is a great piece of email software, but at times they may not be reliable. What you need is a reliable provider that can help you get your message right to your email recipient's inbox.

Just think about this. What happens if you send out an email and it lands in your customer's spam or promotional folder? It's going to be pretty difficult to get a sale from customers who never even see your email. This is what can happen with the email platforms listed above.

But it's not just about the software. There are many things you need to be aware of when launching an email marketing campaign. No worries, though. I am going to make you a master at sending emails.

E-commerce email marketing is very, very different than traditional email marketing. In traditional email marketing, you are taught to personalize your email. You send each email in your name and you are required to wrap stories around it. Now, don't get me wrong. This is absolutely what you must do if you own a blog, a digital product, a course, coaching, or if you are just trying to sell yourself as a brand.

However, for e-commerce, email is very different. You need to have the right mindset. You need to think like you are a Best Buy or an Office Depot. You need to brand yourself as an identity, a store, and send that email with the store name. Even the time at which you send out your emails, whether you do it yourself or have the email scheduled to be automatically sent, is also different.

I know this seems like a lot, and it is not my intention to throw everything at you at once. What I want to do is simplify the entire process of emailing customers for you. I want to share with you my W5 strategy. My W5 strategy consists of who, what, when, where, and why - and it's really quite simple.

Let's start with the who. The who is your brand name. You always want to send your emails from your brand name, so that whenever your customer receives your email, they see your store's name. There is no exception to this rule. When you subscribe to a newsletter from Best Buy, or Staples, Office Depot, or Walmart, you don't ever hear from the CEO or from the founders of the company. Walmart, Best Buy, or Office Depot is always the name in the "From" field of the email. The company or brand is what you subscribe to. Make sure your who is always consistent and is always your brand name.

The second W is what. Your email must answer the customer's question, "What's in it for me?" We talked about this earlier and it bears repeating. Remember, customers are selfish. You need to give them a reason to purchase something from you. You have to tell them what's in it for them if they click the link in the email. It can be free shipping. It can be a free gift. It can be 50% off. It can be a summer sale, a private sale, or a Christmas sale. Always answer "What's in it for me?" first. That's what consumers want. You can also build relationships with your customers by educating them with niche-specific content emails, and by offering products based on your experience.

However, for e-commerce, email is very different. You need to have the right mindset. You need to think like you are a Best Buy or an Office Depot. You need to brand yourself as an identity, a store, and send that email with the store name. Even the time at which you send out your emails, whether you do it yourself or have the email scheduled to be automatically sent, is also different.

I know this seems like a lot, and it is not my intention to throw everything at you at once. What I want to do is simplify the entire process of emailing customers for you. I want to share with you my **W5 strategy**. My W5 strategy consists of **who, what, when, where, and why** - and it's really quite simple.

Let's start with the **who**. The who is your brand name. You always want to send your emails from your brand name, so that whenever your customer receives your email, they see your store's name. There is no exception to this rule. When you subscribe to a newsletter from Best Buy, or Staples, Office Depot, or Walmart, you don't ever hear from the CEO or from the founders of the company. Walmart, Best Buy, or Office Depot is always the name in the "From" field of the email. The company or brand is what you subscribe to. Make sure your who is always consistent and is always your brand name.

The second W is **what**. Your email must answer the customer's question, "What's in it for me?" We talked about this earlier and it bears repeating. Remember, customers are selfish. You need to give them a reason to purchase something from you. You have to tell them what's in it for them if they click the link in the email. It can be free shipping. It can be a free gift. It can be 50% off. It can be a summer sale, a private sale, or a Christmas sale. Always answer "What's in it for me?" first. That's what consumers want. You can also build relationships with your customers by educating them with niche-specific content emails, and by offering products based on your experience.

The third W is **when**. When is very important. You need to make sure you send your emails at a very specific time of the day, and this varies from day to day. When you send emails on any day from Monday to Friday, you want to send it between 9 a.m. and 11 a.m. This is proven to be the perfect window of opportunity. Many internet marketers have tested this time. It has always proven to get the highest open rate, which reflects the number of people who open your emails, as well as the highest click through rate, which is the number of email openers who click a link within your email message.

Weekends are different. First, you never send out an email on a Saturday unless it is urgent, such as if you have a sale that ends on a Sunday and you want to remind your customers about it. But if it is not really desperate, do not touch Saturday. On Sunday, the best time to send out your emails is after 12 noon, because that is when people are getting up, finishing brunch, or getting out of church. It is critical in e-commerce that your emails are sent within these time frames.

The fourth W is **where**. This one is very easy. Where is simply the page of your online store that you want your customer to visit when they click on your email. Don't direct people to your main website or home page. You need a specific landing page created just for your email. If you are running a summer sale and your link sends customers back to the main website where they cannot instantly find information about that sale, then they're gone - and you lose sales.

If you have a specific webpage or landing page that talks about the summer sale featuring products marked down or discounted for that sale, then your chance of a sale is extremely high because you have already pre-filtered these people.

People landed on that page because they saw an offer on the summer sale in your email and chose to click it. They are on that page for the sole purpose of checking out that offer - and to potentially buy the products associated with it. So make sure you know exactly where to send these people. Do not send an email without having a where page in place. Do not send an email without any links. Your email should always give people a link to click that takes them to the sale.

The last W is the why. Why is more for you than for your customers. Why are you sending the emails? What is your goal behind sending each particular email? Is it to increase your sales, to tell people about your best-seller, or to tell people to sign up for a contest? Maybe it is simply to generate email leads.

Choose whatever you want, but you must identify your ultimate goal with each email. Of course, in the end we all know it is about making the sale. But there are times when you need to send out an email just to get more Facebook page subscribers, or because you want people to check out a video for the presale of a new product. Always define - and remember - why you are sending the email.

Now, sales events always work well for your e-commerce business, but you do not want to send an email every single day.

It's true that sending emails doesn't cost you any money. It is the lowest hanging fruit because you don't have to pay for this form of advertising. You don't even have to pay any money to acquire the customer because they are already in your database! All do is send them an email and get them to go to your website and ask for a purchase.

But don't abuse this opportunity. I see many e-commerce websites that send emails almost every day, and I can tell you this. If you send an email every day, people will get annoyed and will unsubscribe from your email. When this happens, you lose that customer forever

Instead, you must strategize your email campaign with an effective schedule.

Once you know what to put in your emails and you have mastered the W5, put a mailing schedule in place. Mailing schedules are very important.

How many emails should you send per week? Three. I have taken the time to test this with my own e-commerce stores and have found that three per week works best.

Do not rush and decide you will send an email out tomorrow. You will have no solid idea of what you should send out and this will hurt your bottom line. To be a smart entrepreneur, to be a smart e-commerce business owner, you need to have a mailing schedule and you should have it made up at least a month in advance. The coming month's schedule should specify the days emails will go out, and the purpose for each email in terms of products, promotions, or strategy. Put this schedule on a calendar and stick to it!

Now, there might come a time when you will run out of products or ideas for messages to send to your customers. If you reach this point and run out of products to promote, or you have an empty mailing slot and don't know what to fill it with, there is a great solution:

Simply sign up as an affiliate for another company, mail out an offer for them, and make a commission. By doing so, you are diversifying your brand and you are making a commission without doing anything extra. It's a win-win situation!

The reality is that being an affiliate is quite similar to inventory arbitrage. You are arbitraging because you just send email traffic to the affiliate offer and let that company take care of handling the sales. All you do is collect your commission money.

Think affiliate sales isn't for you? Think again. It is very important for you to start introducing affiliate offers to your database of customers.

Go to Google.com and look for companies in your niche which have an affiliate program. There will be a ton of options that appear in your search. You can also go to www.clickbank.com or www.offervault.com to find affiliate products in your niche that you can sell.

Follow the W5, have your mailing schedule in place, make sure you are following through and sending emails consistently, and you are guaranteed to multiply your profits right away.

You are now a master of email marketing!

Using McDonald's Strategy To Make More Without Spending More

"Do you want fries with that?"

If you live on this planet, I guarantee you've heard that question many times throughout your life. McDonald's started using this sales technique in the 1970s when they discovered that 200 customers per day were ordering hamburgers without French fries. McDonald's trained its staff to ask, "Do you want fries with that?" whenever someone ordered a burger.

After they implemented this one single question, 50% of their customers started ordering French fries — and their average order value rocketed up. It wasn't long before other retailers started to use this strategy in their businesses to maximize their average order value.

Increasing your average order value is the second profit multiplier strategy.

Average Order Value

Average order value is vital to an e-commerce business. Remember earlier in this book when we were calculating CPA, I told you to optimize your advertisement around your break-even point? Well, average order value is why. Even if you are breaking even with your ad, any "fries" purchased become pure profit for your business. The fact is, the higher your average order value, the more advertising you can afford, and the faster your business can scale.

You can immediately apply several strategies to increase your average order value and make more money. I'm going to share these with you here to help you increase your average order value and to bank more from the same customers who are already buying from you.

Volume Discounts

Volume discounts are used widely by retailers that sell shoes. When you go into a shoe store to buy a pair of shoes, you'll often see "Buy one, get one 50% off." This is a volume play and it's an irresistible offer to consumers. I bet you have fallen into this buying trap. After all, who wants to miss out on a deal?

This same selling technique can be applied to your store. You incentivize customers to buy more than one item from you with a discount based on the quantity they choose. You can set this up with apps from the Shopify App store to give additional discounts if the customer buys 2 or more, or 3 or more, or even 5 or more. This will immediately increase your average order value without spending more on ads.

Upsell

If you go to Best Buy today to buy a brand new smart TV, you'll be asked to buy an extended warranty. That extended warranty is an immediate upsell that increases Best Buy's average order value. It's considered a "no-brainer" product; a product that complements the initial product purchased.

Most of the time, the upsell comes with a discount and huge benefits and is only shown when your customer is about to check out. You need to upsell your customers. By simply adding an additional product to their cart, you have increased your average order value once again.

Coupon

Once again, I'm sure you have seen this in your own purchasing past. You shop at a retail store and the minute you finish paying, the cashier gives you something with your receipt — a coupon valid only on your next purchase.

You might want to strangle the cashier at that moment, but you don't want to miss out either. You go back into the store to buy more, or you save it in your wallet and try not to forget to use it. Use this selling technique in your e-commerce store too: Put a coupon on the receipt page.

As an e-commerce store owner, you want to always be on the lookout for ways to increase your average order value. As I said earlier, the higher your average order value, the more you make. The more you make, the more you can advertise and build a decent sized brand. Many e-commerce businesses fail to do this and that's why they are stuck in their growth. But as a smart e-commerce entrepreneur — which you are now — always ask yourself how you can increase your average order value. At the end of the day, it's money that goes straight into your pocket.

Scaling Up Your Traffic

When you have found a winning product, and you have implemented all the strategies to increase your average order value, it's time to scale up your traffic and scale up your business. There are several ways for you to scale your business and your traffic. I'll share several with you in this book that you can immediately apply to your store once you have found a product that's working for you.

First, scale with Facebook Ads. This is the easiest and fastest way for you to scale. Since you have now tested the market and found a product and targeting that is working, you can now scale on Facebook horizontally and vertically. Vertical scaling simply means increasing the daily budget on the campaign that is producing good results.

Horizontal scaling is also very important. Once you find the initial audience that is working for you, go to Audience Insights within Facebook. This time, enter the targeting that is producing results for you. Then head over to the Page Likes section and create more ad sets targeting the audience that Facebook deems relevant to the one already working for you. Now all you do is test more audiences by creating more ad sets. The ultimate goal when you are scaling on Facebook is to get at least 100 purchases. Then start testing with Lookalikes.

Lookalikes is the most powerful advertising technology I've seen to date. With its advanced technology and data-mining, Facebook can find audiences that are similar to the customers that are buying from you. Lookalikes go from 1% to 10% of the population with similar interests, behaviors, and demographics as your buyers. To scale, just increase the percentage. If you are able to get Lookalikes to convert, you are well on track to build a 7-figure business.

At the same time, don't put all your eggs in one Facebook basket. Start with Facebook first and then diversify your traffic sources. Learn about YouTube ads, Google ads, Bing ads, and other traffic generation techniques that can allow you to keep growing. Remember the Greek Column?

To learn more about other traffic generation and other marketing and optimisation techniques, visit Designate Academy. In a nutshell, once you find something that is working, spend more on advertising. This will result in more sales and more customers for your business.

Instant Investors (PayPal Working Capital) (Applicable if you live in US, UK, Australia or Germany)

The third step to the profit multiplier system is diversification. When you diversify your product line, you ultimately need cash. As they say: In any business, cash is king. The more cash you have, the bigger your business is going to be.

"But I'm just starting out!" you might be thinking. "I don't have a significant amount of cash - and I don't have a line of credit."

I have good news for you.

Let me introduce you to your instant investor. This is not a business partner, a line of credit, or even a personal loan. It's a way to get instant funding at a super low interest rate: less than 3%. I touched upon it earlier. It has to do with the importance of accepting PayPal.

If you are still not accepting PayPal, you are losing a huge opportunity. Honestly, what I am about to show you will knock your socks off.

You see, PayPal works directly with a bank called WebBank. This partnership works to your advantage by instantly providing you with a loan to help you expand your business

"There's no way it's that easy," you say. But it is. The only thing that they look at is the sales within your PayPal account. The beauty is that without a credit check, you can get a loan of up to $97,000 with a flat fee of interest that is just $2000. That's basically 2% interest. You only pay a flat fee with no annual or compound interest.

The application process is very simple. All you do is fill out an application which takes five minutes. As I said above, there is no credit check and you get instant funding. Your funding will be available and in your PayPal account in less than a minute.

Want to hear the best part?

You don't have to worry about repayment because you are still accepting PayPal money from your sales. You can choose to pay off PayPal by giving them a percentage of your sales every single day. You can choose to keep 90% of the sales one day and use only 10% of your sales to pay back your loan, or you can keep 70% of your sales and use 30% to pay back the loan. Obviously, the faster you pay them back, the less your flat-rate interest fee will be.

With this method, you do not need any personal guarantee. There is no early repayment penalty. It is completely unlike credit cards or traditional bank loans, which hit you with higher interest, annual fees, late fees, and often prepayment penalties. These traditional forms of funding demand complicated applications and often take weeks to approve and deposit your funds.

But with PayPal, your working capital is just a couple clicks away!

You can easily get up to $97,000 and invest it into diversifying your product line. But you must accept PayPal to have access to this funding. The minimum requirement for eligibility is to have a PayPal business account for at least three months and process at least $20,000 in sales annually. That's it!

If you meet these requirements, PayPal will lend you money so you can expand your business. It's a beautiful thing.

It's like having direct access to an investor and paying a very small percentage in fees for the funding you need.

Strengthening Your Brand

Now that you know how to get your working capital straight from PayPal, it's time to start considering taking your top-selling products and giving them private labels.

Private labeling simply means that instead of the product packaging bearing the manufacturer's name, the packaging shows the retailer's name. Doing this works to your distinct advantage.

By private labeling your product, you will be able to put your brand name on every package and product you choose. You can work with the same AliExpress vendors. All you need to do is request to buy in bulk quantity and for permission to put your brand name on the products. They will ask you for a minimum order, and that is fine, because now you know exactly how to get your working capital straight from PayPal. You can now invest in these products! You can also go directly to Alibaba.com to source your product.

Not only does private labeling strengthen your brand; it can also lower your costs. In many cases, the vendor will give you a much lower cost-per-unit when you buy in bulk. This increases your profit margin on every order you sell.

But all of this still doesn't mean you have to fill the orders. You can keep the same arrangement that you've had with your vendor. The only difference is that your vendor will supply the products under your brand name, while shipping it out from their location. So you still do not have to worry about the cost of holding inventory.

At this point, you can also utilize the powerful marketing strategy of the personal touch…

Consider including a thank you card or flyer in each product package. Online consumers don't generally expect to receive a thank you card. If that thank you card is handwritten, it really takes their relationship with you to a whole new level. What I do is put a specific coupon code inside the thank you card. I also include a flyer so my customers can see what other products we carry.

When you add this kind of personal touch, the customer thinks, "Wow! I am getting a discount coupon to go and buy other products. I am getting exactly what I ordered. It's not a scam!" What you are doing is building the confidence of your buyers so they will return to your website and buy even more products.

In addition to branding your packages and including thank you cards, it's probably time to invest in customer support to better serve your customers. This is incredibly important; the more happy customers you have, the more sales you will make in the long run.

You might be surprised that even though a consumer starts out by spending a mere $20 in my store, their lifetime customer value can go all the way up to $1,500. Why? Because I have built a customer-centric support team that takes good care of my customers. When a customer sees a toll-free number on your website, it increases your conversion rate. In fact, you will receive phone orders.

When I started building my customer support team and placing a heavier focus on the customer, my sales from phone orders went up. Today, phone orders account for nearly 10% of my regular sales. So if I have a store that sells around $1,500 per day, about $100 to $150 of those come in via phone orders.

Obviously, you won't only take phone orders with your customer support team. You can do much more with this level of manpower. For example, they can call customers with abandoned carts and follow up on those potential sales. You can also provide your customer service team with a compensation package that motivates them to upsell other products when they are on the phone with your customers.

The final brand-strengthening method that I am going to share with you is to get involved with charity. People love it when you give back to the community. When they see a brand that supports a specific charity, they will feel that they are a part of what you are doing. Look at Toms Shoes. Right now, for every shoe Toms sells, they make a pair of the same shoes for underprivileged kids.

Just think about the strength of the message that charity delivers to the public!

People know that whenever they buy a pair of shoes from Toms, another pair of shoes will be donated to someone who needs them. This builds an unrivaled relationship between the company and its customers. When you do this, your customers aren't only happy that they bought something from you; they feel good on a moral level. This is very important. If your customer feels good about buying from you, then you will have a lifetime customer. The value of that will continually grow in terms of money.

Diversifying Your Product Line

When you go into a specific niche and master the first three steps of my 5-Step System, you really want to start moving toward the diversification of your product line as part of your profit multiplier step. Start carrying and shipping products that are indirectly related to what you are currently selling. This way, you can start capturing new audiences and customers.

For example, in a leading online store, they sold water purification products. Water purification is the core of the business, but in order to expand that business they needed to diversify by adding another similar niche of products. This would let them spread out and gain different angles of attack that would allow them to reach out to new audiences and new customers on a daily basis.

Since their main product was in water purification, they started to diversify into the green and home living product line. These really go well with water purification, which is a home product and a green product.

Essentially, they began looking for other green products that would complement their water purification products and change the way people saw their store. Now they have a green line that attracts people who are eco-friendly and want to save money and the environment.

The beauty of this concept is astounding!

These two product lines cross-sell each other. Their water purification customers can buy their green and home living products, and their green and home living customers can buy their water purification products. The products are indirectly related, but still in the same healthy home living niche.

By doing this, they doubled their business because they had mastered the first three steps of this system. All they had to do was apply the first three steps to a new sub-niche. They automatically doubled their business simply by doubling the product lines offered in their store.

Let's look at another fine example of diversification success: **Zappos**.

In the beginning, Tony and Nick decided to target a very specific niche; there were a lot of people with very big feet size who had a difficult time finding shoes that fit. Let me tell you, if you wear a size 18 shoe, it's very hard to find shoes that fit. Tony had discovered an opportunity and he went after that niche market. He then expanded to antique shoes, collectible shoes, and eventually he expanded to offer many different lines of shoes.

Fast forward to today. The company's name has changed to Zappos, and it doesn't just focus on shoes anymore. It has diversified its product line by selling indirectly related products. It now sells apparel, clothing, shorts, sunglasses, and hand bags.

This is how the company started to grow exponentially, by simply diversifying its product line and creating a large portfolio. It was this diversification that attracted Amazon, which was willing to pay billions of dollars to acquire the company.

When diversifying your product line, pay attention to the following tips.

First, don't just carry low-priced items. You should also carry medium- to high-ticket items. This creates diversity in product type as well as product price. For you to have a very successful store, you need to sell items priced from one dollar all the way to $1,500.

This is how you start building more sales and making more profit, because people won't just come to you for products that are under $20. Once they have established a relationship with you and they know your store provides good products that are delivered in a timely manner, they will be more than willing to buy products from you that are hundreds or even thousands of dollars. These consumers will keep coming back to your store to check out and buy what you sell.

Another tip to keep in mind when diversifying: Do not start raking in inventory. Even if you have cash or working capital from PayPal, do not fall into the trap of getting a bunch of inventory to sell. You need to test the market first, and apply the principle of inventory arbitrage to the diversification of your product line.

Simply find another vendor who will drop ship for you. Then you can test products that are indirectly related to your store and determine which products work. If you find a best-seller, then follow Step 4, selling the product under your own brand name. This will minimize your risk and allow you to invest in inventory in a new market without spending a fortune.

My rule of thumb is to start creating your own brand name and have inventory when you can consistently sell 100 units of the same product every day for 30 days in a row. If you have not achieved this minimum requirement, I do not encourage you to even think about creating your own brand and having inventory.

Follow the Facebook strategy I have shared with you and focus on that for your new product line. If you can double your traffic with a new product line, I can virtually guarantee you will double your business within a very short amount of time.

What's Next? Rinse & Repeat

You have made it to the 5th and final step!

Now that you have mastered the first four steps of my 5-Step System, you are ready to focus on the final step, Rinse & Repeat.

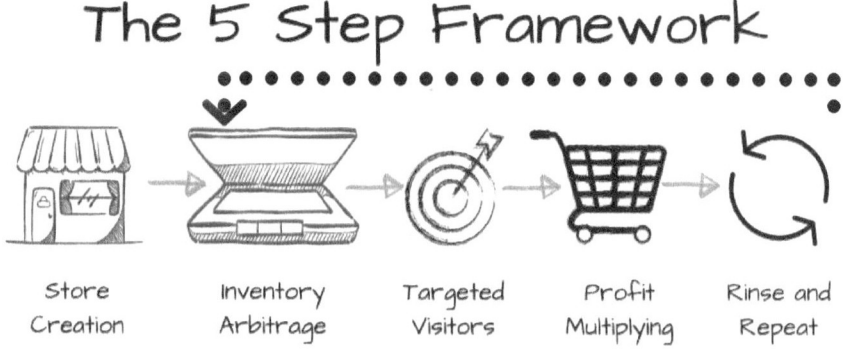

You've gone through the process. You know what to do. When you have one product that generates $500 a day for you, you are experienced in my 5-Step Blueprint. Just repeat the same process that I shared with you in this book to find and sell more winning products. If you can find 3 products that each produce $500 a day for you, that's $1,500 a day right in your pocket. All you're doing is rinsing and repeating.

However, here's an advanced warning on selling multiple products. If you are testing more than one product in your store through Facebook Ads, you must use Pixel Bay to create specific product conversion pixels. The Facebook pixel algorithm is smart, but only if you give it the right information to optimize sales of one product. When you start selling multiple products through Facebook Ads, it will confuse Facebook's pixel and algorithm.

So, while your goal is to rinse and repeat the process to find more products, make sure you tell Facebook specifically which product you want to optimize your ads around, or you will be running around in circles.

Once you have several products that are selling well, you need to start thinking like a real CEO. This might also be the time for you to outsource or to hire an assistant who can handle your initial four steps. There are many places from where you can find and hire a virtual assistant for about $200 a month.

It is at this point that you can truly become a CEO of your business. Being a CEO means that your sole focus is on growth and expansion, while the day-to-day work is handed over to your assistant.

At the same time, focus on automation. This is why I recommended Shopzie earlier in this book. The less time you waste on repeated tasks, the more you'll make and the more time you will have.

When focusing on growth and expansion, leverage your website to attract products with authority. What do I mean by "authority"? I mean products which are well-known in your marketplace. Since by now you will have an extensive portfolio thanks to the four steps you have followed, I can guarantee you will start building a large and responsive database.

You will start to build traffic data and customer data, both important assets. You can create a portfolio or a PowerPoint presentation, and pitch your brand to well-established products within your marketplace. Once you gain approval, you can resell these products in your store.

Some of these well-known products may actually come looking for you as well. Just remember that they want to be sure you are a well-established e-commerce website. By sharing data that demonstrates the large size of your database, and the many visitors to your store, you will pique the interest of products that are very well-known in your industry.

This is the point at which you can start working with innovative new products. You can start working with high-price products. You can work with a lot of vendors that are in the United States and you can sell products that are very well-known.

Once you have created a relationship with a well-established product or company, they will want proof that you can actually sell. To do this, you need to fully utilize your email marketing system to create a spike in sales and wow your new vendors. When your vendors can see your ability to sell, they will bend over backward to do whatever they can to support you. This again strengthens your brand and diversifies your company.

Keep in mind that you simply cannot do any of this if you are still running the day-to-day operations of your business. Get that virtual assistant! Your focus should be entirely on the growth and expansion of your e-commerce store. Once that's all done, you will initiate Rinse & Repeat, which is the fifth step.

Step 5 is super easy! Your goal is to build multiple streams of income. Each e-commerce store is one of those streams. One store might be selling $10,000 a day and another store might be generating only $500. Your third store might be doing $2,000, and your fourth store might be doing $5,000.

Do you see how this is all working?

By diversifying into a different niche or a new brand, you will start making more money by applying the four simple steps to each of these stores.

At this point, you know exactly how to create your website. You know how to strengthen your brand. You know how to inventory arbitrage. You know how to drive traffic to your website. By simply taking these four steps to an entirely new market, you will have more e-commerce stores and can start generating more income.

You will be making money while you are asleep!

Remember, e-commerce operates 24 hours a day, seven day a week, 365 days a year. You are literally making sales night and day. I started with a Coffee business. Now I have a lot more niches and we are looking into creating our own supplement line.

This is how I built multiple sources of income with my companies. If each of them generates $10,000 a day, that adds up to $40,000 in sales every single day! Some of them sell $15,000 and others, $20,000, but it averages out to $40,000 a day with four stores.

What does that mean for me?

That is a total of $14 million in sales per year. Right there is your eight-figure empire by simply Rinsing & Repeating the first four steps within different niches.

This is how you can start to take the knowledge you have learned and the opportunities at your doorstep.

Just execute to start making a ton of cash, and maximize the potential that you have right in front of you!

Flip Your Store Like Real Estate

Your e-commerce store is a revenue-producing asset. Many business owners love to buy assets that continue to produce revenue for them because they can control their returns. This is why business owners love to buy e-commerce businesses. A profitable e-commerce business is a valuable asset and it can be sellable in the future as well.

If you're the type of person who loves to build and sell, you can simply flip your stores like real estate. The more sales your e-commerce business generates, the more you can make selling it. You don't always have to build a legacy business and continue to run it. Instead, you can build an e-commerce business, make it profitable, and then sell it for 25x of your monthly profit. This way you can cash out and build a brand new e-commerce business.

One person in my network created an online swimming gear store — and three months later sold it for $22,000 in cash. If you do this a couple times a year, pocketing $100,000 is very possible. Several online platforms exist to help you find buyers and sell your business: Flippa.com, Latonas.com and EmpireFlipper.com. Even Shopify has Shopify Exchange, designed for e-commerce store owners to sell their stores.

The more revenue and profit your store generates, the higher its sale price will be. This is the beauty of e-commerce. You can create a store and flip it for whatever price that you'd like. Since you know the 5 Steps, you can rinse and repeat in different niches, and continue to create and sell. It is up to you. If creating and flipping sounds like you, then definitely explore this route.

Final Thoughts

CONGRATULATIONS!

If you have applied everything I have taught you in this book and you have hustled to create your e-commerce store, you will start generating profits in a very short amount of time.

As for those of you who are reading this book and did not do a single thing I told you, tell me one thing:

What the hell are you waiting for?

I encourage you to go back to the beginning of this book right now. Re-read the entire thing, applying everything.

I have shared with you a lifetime's worth of my discoveries, tests, trials, and the millions of dollars I have spent to discover this proven 5-Step Framework. I have given it to you flat out. If you are not hustling... if you are still dreaming and not taking action, then you will never succeed online.

The fact is that you are just one step away from being a successful entrepreneur. Screw 9-5 jobs! Screw working for minimum wage! Screw working in a box! Screw working at jobs you don't like!

I have just handed you an opportunity. I just gave you the full 5-Step System! If this doesn't excite you, I don't know what else possibly can. I don't know what else I could give you that would prompt you to start building your first business.

There's a saying I must have used a zillion times in my life to push myself out of the fear of grabbing opportunities like these:

"You don't say No to a million dollar lottery just because you have a salary"

If you don't take action, you will regret it because the opportunity will soon vanish. It is right now that we are at the peak of e-commerce. If you don't ride the wave before everyone else moves to e-commerce, you will miss your chance. The market is going to become saturated. At that point, when you look back on the opportunity that this 5-Step System offered, you will regret that you did not take action.

Do it! Give up your TV time! Create a rhythm to work on your new business. By allocating just one to two hours, you can have your e-commerce business up and running in less than 30 days - and start generating profit. That's all you need.

Please don't let this book just sit on your bookshelf or coffee table collecting dust. I want to empower you! I want to change your life! In fact, I want to change the life of every single person who is reading this book.

I wrote this book only to give you this opportunity. I firmly believe that every single person should be given this opportunity

But you need to take action!

Now, I want to hear from you. I want to hear your success stories. Email me directly, any time, at Hola@thedesignate.xyz and tell me that you are already becoming a successful entrepreneur, that you are already making money online, and that you left your job to create the financial reality of which your dreams. Follow me on social media and direct message me your story. I love hearing your stories and seeing other people succeed using my methods.

That's really all I care about!

Finally, I want to thank you from the bottom of my heart for reading this book and applying the treasured information inside it. I really do hope you enjoyed this book.

Last, but not least, please take action. I believe you are an entrepreneur. Every single individual reading this book is an entrepreneur. The only difference between successful people and unsuccessful people is opportunity, knowledge, and execution. I just gave you all three of those, right inside this book.

Use it!

Thank you For
Reading